Protecting Moscow from the Soviets

And Other Stories

Also By Peter Baird:
Beyond Peleliu, a novel
(Ravenhawk Books)

Protecting Moscow from the Soviets

And Other Stories From:

The New York Times Magazine
Newsweek
The Wall Street Journal
Men's Health
The Chicago Tribune Magazine
The Cleveland Plain Dealer Magazine
The Arizona Republic
Phoenix Magazine
The Scottsdale Progress
Arizona Attorney
Rosebud
Interrace Magazine
Writer's Digest Magazine
Litigation Magazine

Shark Tales
(Simon & Schuster)

Criminology (Second Edition)
(Harcourt Brace Jovanovich)

My Brush With History
(Black Dog & Leventhal)

Signs of Hope
(Pushcart Press)

Beyond Peleliu
(RavenHawk Books)

Peter Baird

Protecting Moscow from the Soviets: And Other Stories
by Peter Baird

ISBN 13: 978-0-88100-143-3
ISBN 10: 0-88100-143-0

Library of Congress Number: 2008925498

Cover and Book Design: Nick Zelinger, NZ Graphics

Published by
National Writers Press

Printed in the United States of America
First Edition

Library of Congress Cataloging-in-Publication Data:

Baird, Peter.
    Protecting Moscow from the Soviets: a collection of essays/ by Peter Baird
    International Standard Book Number (ISBN) 10: 0-88100-143-0
    International Standard Book Number (ISBN) 13: 978-0-88100-143-3

    1. Literary Collections/General/American   2. Literary Collections/Essays
    3. Social Science/Essays   4. Family & Relationships
    5. Law/Essays   I. Title   2008925498

For Susanne, again

Acknowledgements

This collection would not exist without the relentless efforts of my agent, Andy Whelchel; the secretarial toils of Anita Smedley and Susan Walker; the editorial skills of Stephanie Kane and Kimberly Demarchi; the support of my partners, associates and staff at the Lewis and Roca LLP law firm; and the ever-present encouragement of my wife, Susanne Marie Mercier Baird.

"*If he wrote about it, he could get rid of it.*
He had gotten rid of many things by writing them."

~ Ernest Hemingway,
Winner Take Nothing "Fathers and Sons" (1933)

PREFACE

My favorite cartoon has two men on a street corner and one says to the other, "Well enough about me. How did you like my new book?"

Those words would be even funnier if I were to say them because this book is "about me." More generally, it is about the lives and experiences that my characters and I have had in fact, fiction and memory.

The pieces in this collection were written over a twenty-five year period and they are as different from one another as appearing before the United States Supreme Court is from fighting the Japanese during World War Two, as battling polio is from watching sex videos and as a Christmas Eve Mass is from a Las Vegas magic show.

Some chapters come from publications as familiar as *Newsweek*. Others come from publications as obscure as *Interrace*. Several were rescued from my towering mountain of unpublished, unfinished and rejected manuscripts. And the book excerpt is from my novel, *Beyond Peleliu*.

I have tried to make the facts as accurate as memory would permit and the fiction as inventive as imagination would allow. The errors are all mine.

Peter D. Baird
Phoenix, Arizona
June, 2008

CONTENTS

CHAPTER THREE: FAMILY MAN
WIVES, KIDS, COPS AND SEX VIDEOS

CHAPTER FOUR: WRITER
SHORT FICTION, LONG FICTION AND LITERARY REJECTION

CHAPTER FIVE: CLIENTS, CAUSES AND CASES
FREEDOM OF SPEECH, FREEDOM OF RELIGION
AND THE RIGHT TO REMAIN SILENT

CHAPTER SIX: LAWYER
MIND, MAGIC AND MISTAKES

CHAPTER ONE

GROWING UP

THE COLD WAR, MAGIC, MUSIC, MOTHER AND POLIO

Protecting Moscow From The Soviets

Real Magic

The Leg That Didn't Work

Forever Mamma

"The Evening Breeze Caressed The Trees"

Protecting Moscow From the Soviets

Delta-Bravo-Zero-Four-Black were our code words in Moscow that summer of 1954. The Cold War was on, and, despite our adolescence, we were right in the middle of it. Armed with Defense Department charts that showed the silhouettes, names, ranges, and blood-red stars of Soviet military aircraft, we scanned the skies and reported any unidentified sightings to our uniformed handlers at Fairchild Air Force Base. We peered through government-issue binoculars, watching for a sneak attack on Moscow — a small rural, college town surrounded by contoured wheat fields in the panhandle of northern Idaho.

We belonged to the Air Force Ground Observer Corps and were among 375,000 Americans who, in organized shifts, monitored horizons all over the country, reporting directly to the Air Force. According to the promotional materials from the Defense Department, the Soviets had the bomb and the planes to drop it, but America's DEW line — the distant early-warning-radar-system — could not reliably detect low-flying bombers and their escort MiGs, especially in the Pacific Northwest where we lived. With the United States so vulnerable, the Air Force operated the Ground Observer Corps for some nine years in the 1950s, enlisting private citizens to operate observation posts and act, it was said, like modern-day Paul Reveres.

Between the seventh and eight grades, when Doris Day was singing "Secret Love" on the radio and adults were talking about the Army-McCarthy hearings at the dinner table, members of my Boy Scout Buffalo Patrol took our first loyalty oath, promising not to overthrow our government, and were formally inducted into the Ground Observer Corps. From the Air Force recruiter came promises of shiny silver wing pins, a subscription to *Aircraft Flash* magazine for photos of military jets with billowing contrails, and viewings of fun Air Force movies about the earth slowly turning red, like a Sherwin-Williams paint commercial.

A more effective pitch came from veteran sky watchers in our scout troop. Hidden behind the Soviet-aircraft identification chart in the observation shack was, we were told, a legendary book containing unprecedented carnal scenes not found in any available literature of the day. But that was not all. Supposedly the fastest girl in the eighth grade had signed up for the Ground Observer Corps, giving titillated Buffaloes all manner of sexual double entendres to snicker about when discussing the observation shack.

Because of where we lived, it didn't take much to recruit us. According to adolescent folklore, Moscow, Idaho, was unquestionably the number-one Soviet bombing target. Although the town's high school team was the Bears and one of its colors was red and there was even an annual May Day parade led by obscure Hollywood actors almost everyone pretended to have heard of, there were not, to our immense pride, any real similarities between the Moscow in Idaho and the other one. After all, we were the free Moscow, and that comparative fact was always cabled to the Kremlin as part of our May Day festivities, baiting the Reds and brazenly giving them yet another reason to obliterate a small Idaho town first. There was another crucial difference: unlike the Russian Moscow, ours openly celebrated Christmas and did so once with a large banner over Main Street that read, with undetected irony, "Put Christ Back into Christmas-the Moscow Chamber of Commerce."

We began our patriotic observations after a perfunctory training session at the volunteer fire department, and once a week we climbed three flights of stairs, up a ladder, and through a trap door into an unfinished plywood shack on top of Whitworth Junior High School, one of the highest points in town. Overlooking an orderly grid of wide streets, thick maple trees, and quiet middle-class homes, the shack came furnished with one set of perpetually unfocused binoculars, a Soviet-aircraft identification chart, a log book for sign-ins and sightings, and a direct phone line to Fairchild Air Force Base in Spokane.

On duty for the first time in the observation shack, the Buffaloes hastily found the dirty book beneath the Soviet-aircraft identification chart. Even more quickly, we riffled straight to the dog-eared pages, which, though utterly unremarkable by current standards, were enough in those days to draw pubescent patriots up three flights of stairs and a ladder and into four hours of weekly service to their country. To the collective regret of all the Buffaloes, however, the other sign-up incentive proved to be a hoax: except for brief glimpses of her in a rakish Chevrolet driven by a high school boy with glistening black hair, we never saw the alluring eighth-grade girl anywhere that summer.

Once, after weeks of tedium atop Whitworth Junior High School doing nothing more for America than watching crop dusters drone overhead it happened: I spotted what had to be a Soviet MiG, streaking low across the distant fields. Frantic to confirm my sighting, I grabbed the binoculars, slammed them to my sockets, and furiously twisted the infernal focus knob. Sure of what in reality was only an indistinct, fast-moving speck, I called Fairchild Air Force Base, blurted, "Delta-Bravo-Zero-Four-Black," and reported my observation with as much technical jargon as I could hurriedly read from the Soviet-aircraft identification chart, which was not, at the moment, hiding the dirty book.

"O.K., kid, we'll scramble," came the laconic reply. Hyperventilating, I leaped outside to the railing and watched intently for the F-94C Lockheed "Starfires" that our trainers had promised. Squinting, listening, straining, I waited. But, as the minutes dragged on, the Starfires never came. Neither did anything else, except for some wounding stabs of humiliation. After slowly putting the dirty book back into its well-publicized hiding place and then signing the log book without any mention of the debatable MiG or the promised scramble, I left the observation shack and the Ground Observer Corps for good.

A few weeks later I returned to Whitworth Junior High School, not to read dirty books or to watch for Soviet aircraft but to attend eighth grade.

Back in school, I read in my issue of *Junior Scholastic* about a revolutionary new Supreme Court case that had banned something called racial segregation. There was also a newsreel about a Communist military victory over the French in a part of the world that I had never heard of before: Indochina, at a place called Dien Bien Phu. My personal Cold War was over. Other, more difficult battles loomed unseen.

Real Magic

World War Two was great fun for a five-year-old boy like me. My father was off fighting the Japanese and would not come back to fight his personal wars for several years. After he shipped out from California, my mother and I moved to Illinois where we lived with her parents in a Victorian two-story house that overlooked the soupy Illinois River, faced a tree-lined brick street and bordered an industrial area where radium was painted on watch dials so they would glow in the dark.

Summer mornings were for waiting on an occasional, censored letter from the South Pacific and afternoons were for watching barges and warships float downstream toward the Mississippi. At night, I caught fireflies, listened to my grandfather's fables about anthropomorphic rabbits and, best of all, I did magic with my mother.

She was a diminutive woman with deeply expressive eyes and was as engaged by the empirical as she was fascinated by the transcendent. At times, she could be a hard-headed, bustling career woman. At others, she had the ethereal visage of a fairy godmother.

Long before she met my father, my mother had earned a Master's Degree from Northwestern University and had worked as a social worker at an Illinois Women's prison, then at Hull House in Chicago, and later at a girl's club in New York. Along the way, she encountered worldly kids who could pick pockets, cheat at cards, and exploit swindles, scams and sleights of hand. Without even trying, my mother became an amateur magician.

At first, she taught me the "disappearing boy" trick. It was ridiculous. Shutting my eyes and contorting my face, I would "disappear" until she asked, "Where did that boy go?" At those words, my eyes would flash open and, for at least the first seven hundred performances, she would laugh and exclaim, "There he is!"

When I was a little older, she did the "magic rock" trick, which was more complicated than the "disappearing boy" spoof but not much. In the morning, I would pick out a "magic rock" from the river bank; it would remain "in plain view" all day; after dinner, my mother would take me outside on the lawn and, under cover of darkness, she would ditch the rock and then pretended to throw it into the night sky where it "vanished" and never came down. Amazing.

After the last trick of the evening, it was usually time for the adults to listen to the radio and for me to go upstairs to bed. At the first commercial break, my mother would come up to tuck me in and say goodnight. Each time, I would ask how she "did it" and, invariably, she would answer, "it's real magic," and then slowly walk away, smiling.

In time, the war ended; my father returned; and the three of us moved to southern Utah where he was a country doctor in a Mormon farming town and where our crank telephone rang almost non-stop from people needing medical care. It was there, in the late 1940's, that I bought my first magic tricks from a traveling, wood-paneled novelty shop that came down from Salt Lake City to sell country kids whoopee cushions, hand buzzers, itching power and, best of all, conjuring books and gimmicks.

After some practice, I could make a small black ball disappear in the top of a red plastic vase and pull marked cards from a tapered "stripper" deck. Using sleight-of-hand moves, I also perfected a con game called "three card monte" and suckered my little friends into selecting one of three cards, watching me deal each card face down, and identifying the chosen card until they placed a bet on whether they could do it again, which, of course, they couldn't because I had secretly switched cards.

At our house, magic was not just for kids. My mother and I did a two-person "mind-reading" act which she called "black magic" and which we performed for adults as well as for kids. With a room full of people, I would leave and she would stay; someone would silently point to an object in the room; I would return not knowing what the selected object was; my mother would then ask me questions, such as whether "that green ashtray" or "that brown bible" was the chosen object; and, each time, I would say "no." However, when she used our code and asked me about something colored black, I knew that her next question would identify the selected object and that my next answer should be "yes."

Almost always, our "ESP" act evoked stunned silence, audible gasps, and then choruses of "how did you do that?" Invariably, she would say "it's real magic" and slowly walk away, smiling. From my perspective, she was better than Houdini, Blackstone or Dunninger.

Even my father did magic. At holiday parties, he amazed our guests by draping a handkerchief over his hand, burying a lighted cigarette in it, tossing it to a spectator and showing that the cigarette had disappeared without burning, charring or marking the handkerchief in any way. With a twenty-five cent false thumb, he fooled everybody.

Eventually, my father started to wage his own personal wars. His weapons were drinking, philandering, brow-beating and battering. Maybe he was exhausted from being on call 24 hours a day; perhaps his mother-less, semi-orphaned childhood eventually took its emotional toll. More likely, he suffered from an undiagnosed, untreated case of post-traumatic stress disorder syndrome from a gunshot wound he sustained during the World War Two Battle of Peleliu.

Yet, no matter how bad things got at home, we had magic. When my father would get drunk and go on a rampage, my mother and I would retreat to the basement guest room, lock the door, close our eyes and do the "disappearing mother and son trick." After 15 or 20 minutes of quiet, we "reappeared" and things would be better.

Eventually, we left my father, moved back to my mother's parents' home in Illinois and took magic with us. During that summer, I had a respectable cash flow from performing the three-card monte routine for a new crop of neighborhood suckers. Meanwhile, my mother did magic too but it was very different and involved reading books about South America, "disappearing" with her eyes closed for hours and spending long nights at the typewriter.

Finally, my mother announced at a family gathering that she "had been away, traveling in Uruguay." We were stupefied. Whereupon, she went up to her bedroom and came back downstairs with a smudgy stack of typewritten pages and laid it on the table. It was, she told us, a travelogue about a fictitious vacation that my mother and father and I had taken to Uruguay over the course of the summer we had been separated from my father.

With minute detail, she had fabricated a train trip through Uruguay, describing missed connections, endless cathedrals, crazy accommodations, unpronounceable food, mechanical breakdowns, language barriers, intestinal maladies, lost luggage and bizarre misadventures. Her book was built around the unreliable, rickety but always colorful Uruguayan national railway system — the "Administracion de los Ferrocarriles del Estado." However, what gave her story its humorous punch were the invented anecdotes about my father's crankiness with anything foreign, exotic, Catholic, or, for that matter, different.

That fall, my parents reconciled and my mother and I left the fireflies, brick street, radium plant and Illinois River and returned to Utah. A few months later, my mother received The Utah State Book Award for her Uruguayan travelogue and then, as planned, the three of us moved permanently to northern Idaho. Once there, my father mellowed and, whether it was from growing up near the radium plant or losing her immune system to the stress of a stormy marriage, my mother came down with breast cancer.

After her radical mastectomy, my mother's physicians were pessimistic and gave her only a few more months to live. Then, with the help of a nun who was a nurse at the Sacred Heart Hospital, my mother learned to visualize her blood cells destroying the cancer cells. Rather than becoming invisible or traveling to Uruguay or doing a mind reading act with me, she would now close her eyes and cleanse her body of cancer. Despite his doctorly skepticism, my father supported her mental imaging and became an around-the-clock nurse, orderly, cook and housekeeper.

Although my mother lived for years rather than months, the time eventually came for her to go. After losing the power to speak and knowing that she would soon lose her mind, she signaled her readiness for the most transcendent moment of all. On July 7, 1960, in a rural hospital in northern Idaho and with an injection from my father, she did the "disappearing mother" trick, closed her eyes and became invisible, forever.

Today, I am an amateur magician myself and have my own show called, "Illusions of the Mind." After each performance, people regularly come up to me and ask the same questions. "How did you become a magician?" "Why do all the fees from your shows go to cancer research?" And, of course, the most persistent question of all, "How did you do it?"

Invariably, I tell them, "it's real magic." Then I slowly walk away, smiling.

The Leg That Didn't Work

On Christmas Day 1950, I came down with a low-grade fever, headache, sore throat and stiff neck. After I told my physician-father about these flu-like symptoms, he diagnosed my condition as the "Christmas crud" and dispatched me to the medicine cabinet for an aspirin.

Although these symptoms continued into New Year's Day, I barely noticed them because they were mild and also because Christmas was nearly perfect that year. Our rural Utah town was snowed-in. My parents had declared a holiday truce and, under the tree, was an Adams Magic Set that included "Chinese linking rings," a floating wand, a "stripper" deck of cards and the disappearing ball-in-vase trick. For a ten-year-old boy, Christmas was, as we used to say, "the berries."

At about 7:00 a.m. on the morning of January 2, 1951, I awoke to an argument going on down the hall in the kitchen. My father was shouting and my mother was crying — sure signs that the holiday truce was over and that I should get off to school before being sucked into the conflict.

As I was about to pull back the covers, I realized that the top and bottom sheets were soaked with sweat. My neck was as stiff as a gun barrel and my head felt as if a railroad spike had been pounded through my forehead and into the center of my brain. Obviously, the "Christmas crud" had gotten worse.

Slowly, I sat up, swung my legs over the side of an old-fashioned, high-legged bed and, hesitating for a moment because of sudden dizziness, I dropped into my customary free fall. When my feet hit the cold, green-patterned linoleum, a burst of electrifying pain shot through the entire length of my right leg, which immediately buckled and sent me crashing face-first against the night stand and into a tangled heap next to my dresser.

After I hit the floor, I started to cry but, remembering my father's "no cry" rule, I choked back the tears. My nose bled from hitting the nightstand but, at first, I didn't notice. All I could think about was to leave the house and avoid the fracas in the kitchen.

Quickly, I pulled my legs underneath me, tried to stand up but, again, my right leg exploded with pain and I fell back onto the linoleum. Instead of moving as I consciously directed, my right leg had become an immobilized dead-weight but one with live nerves that, against the slightest pressure, ignited bolts of high-voltage excruciation. Something was wrong and, despite an urgent desire to avoid my warring parents, I had to tell my father what had happened.

Dragging my right leg and dripping blood from my nose at the same time, I crawled on my hands and one knee out of the bedroom, through a half bathroom and into the den where my father always parked his black leather doctor's bag and where he would pass on his way to the garage, car and hospital. On the den floor, I pinched my nose to stop the bleeding and heard the approaching clomps of a large, angry man.

When my father walked in, he stopped, gave me a stupefied look and barked, "What in the hell are you doing down there?"

"I can't walk, dad. My right leg is on fire whenever I put any weight on it." At that moment, I lost my composure and started sputtering blood and tears down the front of my pajamas.

Furious at my mother and obviously in a hurry, he shook his head at the sight of his pathetic ten-year-old son lying on the floor with a simple nosebleed and blubbering like a baby. With a jerk, he grabbed up his doctor's bag and said, "Dear God, you're just like your mother. Cry and complain, cry and complain." He evidently thought that I was malingering and trying to get an extra day of Christmas vacation because he said, "Stop the tears, plug the nose, get on your feet and get off to school!" With that, he stormed out the door and, moments later, I heard his Chrysler New Yorker start up, back out and screech off in the direction of the hospital.

Several hours later, a physician and family friend from a neighboring town was at my bedside, taking my temperature, listening through a stethoscope, testing leg reflexes with a rubber mallet and trying to get a history from a patient who, by then, could barely talk or keep his eyes open. "It's polio, he told my mother.

"Oh no!"

"Pete's got the classic symptoms: a severe headache; stiff neck; drenching perspiration; fever of over 102°; elevated pulse; extreme drowsiness; and one limb that's paralyzed."

"But it's winter," my mother said. "Isn't polio a summer disease?"

"It happens mostly in the summer, you're right. But infantile paralysis can strike at any time."

The doctor eased himself off the bed and stood up. "Only his right leg is paralyzed, so Pete probably has spinal polio, which is asymmetrical and attacks just one side of the body at a time."

"That's not the worst kind, then?"

"No, he's not having any trouble breathing and there doesn't appear to be any respiratory dysfunction and so he probably doesn't have the bulbar or the encephalitic forms that attack not just the spinal cord but also the brain." He took a long breath and then added some unnecessary information that he immediately regretted: "In extreme cases, the bulbar and encephalitic forms can kill in a day or two or leave the patient in an iron lung, on crutches or in a wheelchair, sometimes for life."

Hearing those horribles, my mother started to cry and, quickly, the doctor reassured her, "*I don't think* Pete's got either the bulbar or encephalitic. *Please* listen to me."

"Will he ever walk again?," she sobbed.

"Probably. We'll know in about three months. The odds are in his favor."

She leaned against the portly doctor and wept. He patted her on the back and, in a soothing voice, described what the course of my treatment would be. "The first thing we'll do is get some antibiotics into him because, even if polio doesn't get him, pneumonia might. Right now, he's extremely vulnerable to secondary infections."

"What about the paralysis?"

"We used to immobilize kids' limbs in casts and splints but we don't do that anymore." As he hoisted up his doctor's bag, he said, "since he's got to be quarantined anyway, we'll keep him right here; we'll get around-the-clock nurses; and we'll aggressively treat him with the Sister Kenny method." As he left, the doctor told my mother, "Hover, and I'll go to the hospital and talk to his dad."

Although I had never heard of Sister Kenny before, she was then one of the most famous women in America and had been featured in the *Saturday Evening Post, Reader's Digest* and even in a 1946 Hollywood movie called, "Sister Kenny." She was an Australian nurse who lived in Minnesota during the 1940's and she had revolutionized the treatment of infantile paralysis by administering heat and manipulation to afflicted limbs rather than immobilizing them in rigid casts, splints and corsets as the medical establishment traditionally had done.

I'm vague about what happened over the next several months because I slept almost all the time. However, what I do remember, vividly, was the Godawful heat because Sister Kenny's idea of heat was not the under-the-covers cozy type or the middle-of-July sweaty type. Rather, her heat was the kind that burned and blistered and it came in two forms, dry and wet. The dry heat was administered in bed from water bottles so hot that the nurses needed gloves to carry them. The wet heat was administered in the bathtub and the water was often so steamy I could barely make out the faucets.

When the bathtub treatments started, my mother gave me several plastic ducks, fish and boats she apparently hoped would take my mind off the heat. As it turned out, the toys didn't take my mind off anything but they were useful because, whenever the toys got rubbery, the nurses deemed the water to be too hot, even for me.

And so it went as a sleepless mother, chagrined father, and battery of nurses administered heat, salt tablets, skin balms, aspirin, fluids, foot support, blankets, and manipulation. To control the possibility of a secondary bacterial infection, they forced me to swallow giant pills, gold-colored chokers called Aureomycin. Through it all, the best medicine was the marital harmony that polio had fostered between my parents.

Eventually, the heat, Aureomycin, sleep, physical therapy and loving parents worked and, by the time the snow had disappeared outside my bedroom window and the robins had returned to Utah, I took the first, halting steps on my own power down our hallway. Watching with their breaths held until I reached my father's open arms, my parents applauded, cheered, and cried. They had never looked happier. After a few more months of rest and physical therapy, I had recovered and thought, for good reason, that polio was forever behind me.

As it turned out, I was wrong. When I was about to turn 60, I started to experience blurred vision in my right eye. It wasn't all that bad but it persisted despite drops, injections, pills and ever-stronger trifocals. Eventually, I saw an ophthalmological neurologist who, after an MRI and a battery of tests, diagnosed my condition as "post-polio syndrome," "PPS" or "polio bounceback" and prescribed B-12 shots that didn't help.

Evidently, there are between 200,000 and 300,000 polio survivors like me from those pre-Salk vaccine days and, decades after our initial bouts with polio, some of us are experiencing debilitating fatigue, difficulty breathing, muscle atrophy, joint pain and, in some instances, blurred vision. What makes this syndrome so unfair is that it hits those hardest who had the worst original cases — those in wheelchairs or on respirators, crutches, or braces. Indeed, the worldwide web and the literature are filled with heart-breaking accounts of polio survivors whose PPS symptoms have often been misdiagnosed and whose bodies have been degraded, yet again, by the virus.

I was a lucky boy and, 50 years later, I am a lucky man. Today, I only have two reminders of the disease. When I read, watch television or drive at night, I squint to focus. When I get out of bed in the morning, I stand up very slowly.

Forever Mamma

So many people are coming out of closets these days that I suppose it's my turn for a public unburdening. Here it is: now in my mid-50's, I'm becoming a mamma's boy.

Mind you, I didn't say mom or mother and I didn't say son or only child, either. No, I said "mamma" and "boy" and I don't care anymore how pantywaisted those two words may sound. Indeed, if Alzheimer's had left my 87-year-old father with anything more than volcanic rages and a surprisingly dangerous right cross, I would tell him that his taunts from the 1950's have come true, that I'm not a man's man anymore, and, best of all, that I have never felt better in my life.

To put my uncloseted confession into perspective, I'm not a wet-nursed, limp-wristed milquetoast but rather a weathered trial lawyer who has fought through uncounted court cases and, in other contexts, has battled for money as a provider, for grades as a student and for victory as an athlete and coach. At this stage of life, being a mamma's boy means that, for the first time since my mother died over 37 years ago, I'm finally listening to her, taking seriously what she said, and changing.

If my memory is accurate, then I probably stopped paying attention to her advice at about the time I first used the word, "mom," back in 1957. For the previous sixteen years, she had been "mamma" — an organically textured word with a strong, earthy resonance but one which, when enunciated slowly with both syllables flattened out, sounds like the plaintive cry from an unhappy baby. Because of that infantile association, I drew "baby-cakes" snickers from my teenaged friends and "you're-a-sissy" looks from my oversized father no matter how adult or clipped my pronunciation of "mamma" was.

Faced with that combination of peer and paternal pressure, I dropped "mamma" and adopted "mom" — a tight-sounding word which, at least back then, lacked the loamy feel of "mamma" and which often carried with it a sense of tidy aloofness and perfect respectability. Quite apart from my friends' noises and my father's frowns, Rick and Dave Nelson didn't call Harriet "mamma" on the *Ozzie and Harriet* television show and Margaret Anderson was always "mom" to Kathy, Bud and Betty on *Father Knows Best*. Besides, my mother baked pies, wore aprons, kept house and, as was expected in those days, gritted her way through my father's demanding medical practice, episodes of boozy violence, and sporadic indiscretions with a neighbor.

Yet, the momly mold did not fit. She had too many demonstrative, risk-taking, characteristics for that designation; too few suburban orthodoxies for the neighbors; no opinionless dittos for her husband; and precious few fawnings for her son. With energy that seemed at times almost radioactive, she was an amateur magician who was not too proud to give rinky-dink magic shows for little kids; a social worker who had served outcasts in a Chicago settlement house and in Illinois womens' prisons; an odds-minded gambler who, after each visit to Las Vegas, lugged away small, cloth flour bags of silver dollars; a dreamer who loved to watch cloud formations, listen to Verdi and fish for trout; a cancer patient who broke medical conventions of the day by visualizing good cells killing bad ones and who exceeded medical predictions by living an extra three years; and an inveterate writer who, in long-hand, constantly sent letters to her friends, me, and herself, and who even won a literary prize for a travelogue about Uruguay — a country she had never visited. More than anything else, though, she was a teacher who could have enriched more than three decades of my life had she stayed a mamma, and had I only remembered.

To my embarrassment, I tuned her out for the same reason that I changed her name from "mamma" to "mom" — cowardice. It sounds like a contradiction but I became a seemingly tough, ferociously competitive man, not out of confidence or out of courage but out of fear. During my adolescent years, I lived in gutless dread of what my six-foot-two-inch, combat-veteran father might do with his limitless anger if I crossed him or if I didn't do what he demanded.

Consequently, while "mom" battled her way through cancer surgeries and radiation therapies, my father bombarded me with edicts that I did not have the strength, Oedipal or otherwise, to resist. Day in and day out, he pounded me with time-tested orders that had been passed down from his father and from his father's father, such as "never need an eraser;" "do it right the first time;" "don't be a puff;" "win;" "use your head;" "don't cry;" "never quit;" "hit first;" "work like hell;" "never back off;" "fight to the finish;" and the all-purpose, "be a man."

To be fair, those hard-nosed doctrines probably got me through my mother's funeral without shedding a tear and they may even have goaded me into some academic, athletic, and professional successes that, today, look impressive on my resume. But his tough talk did not help me preserve a 27-year marriage, reduce high blood pressure, understand children, be patient, find peace, sleep without nightmares, give love or live without destructive compulsions and crippling inhibitions. And they were no damn good during 20 years of chronic depression, five psychiatrists, and thousands of lithium, Prozac, Paxil and Zoloft pills.

As if recorded on a tape deck surgically implanted in my brain, my father's fierce commands played on for years, drowning out other voices, blocking out other values and slowly turning a specific fear of father into a general fear of failure and then into a relentless perfectionism in which enough was never enough and the most was not enough either. Not until the depression had lifted could I think of her as someone real, hear her voice again, and make her in memory what she had once been in life — human, wise and accessible.

Her insights may not have been original with her but that doesn't matter. What counts is that, for the first time since 1957, I'm remembering, listening, learning and feeling better.

She'd say, "close your eyes and you'll be invisible." Although I had watched mamma close her eyes and act invisible when my father had chased too many jiggers of bourbon with too many bottles of beer, I usually laughed those words off as the remnant of "the disappearing boy trick" she had taught me when I was three or four years old, and actually believed that my body vanished if my eyes were shut. What I didn't understand back then is that, when one's eyes are closed, personal essence does disappear from sight and, invisibly, it can go anywhere and do anything and that those unfettered flights can lead to unseen truths, emotional peace and even physical health. These days, I close my eyes a lot.

From mamma came, "think through your skin." From my father came, "use your head." Taking my cues from him, I used my head all the time, toiling away on academics, ignoring instinct, treating athletics more as a mind game than as physical fun, and living life as if it were a giant SAT examination. In the long run, though, the only person I outsmarted was myself because, as I've learned the hard way, real wisdom does not march out in formation from above the neck on command; rather, it ferments down deep in the body's juices, it sloshes around without the conscious mind even being engaged and then it seeps out through the skin at unpredictable rates and times. It's called "feeling," or, more currently, "emotional intelligence."

"Believe in magic," mamma said. Since she was an amateur magician, I misunderstood her and thought what she wanted was for me to do magic tricks. Consequently, I practiced sleight-of-hand moves like "French drops," "Hindu shuffles," "Elmsley counts," "passes," "forces and "side-slips" and gave my own rinky-dink magic shows for kids in the neighborhood. But I didn't get it. For mamma, magic was not just the secret of a theatrical illusion; it was a life-enhancing metaphor that can propel us beyond the conventional and into the transcendent. These days, I am open to almost anything.

When my father barked, "BE A MAN!," she would amend his order with, "be a man but stay a boy." At long last, I know what she meant. If necessary, I still slug it out, work around-the-clock and fight to the finish for clients, principles and those I love. But today, my battles have limits — beginnings, ends, times, and places. No longer does everything involve winning, getting ahead, proving something, making money, or not losing. Besides the man stuff, I now do the boy stuff, like count clouds; raise dogs; skip stones; feed hummingbirds; watch trains; go fishing; give my own rinky-dink magic shows; and close my eyes to be invisible.

Yet, mamma's wisdom didn't just pop back into my head *un bel di*. Far from it. She had been buried within me for so long as the picture-perfect, 1950's "mom" that I had forgotten what she had really been like and what she had tried to teach me. Worse still, I had lost the ability to look inside myself for her or, sadly, for anything else. After decades of following my father's dictates, taking on my clients' causes, adopting my wife's values and trying to put my children's interests ahead of my own, I had become a man who lived life from the outside in and whose soul was little more than silly putty. No wonder I was depressed.

Finally, in the occluding darkness of my late 40's and early 50's, a physician opened my eyes to who I had become and medication lifted the toxic fog of depression. At the same time, I started to do what mamma herself had done and began writing, not to recount what was external and remembered but to explore what was internal and forgotten.

Without using a computer or a typewriter and without worrying about punctuation, syntax, spelling, grammar, organization, accuracy or even conscious thinking, I mined my subconscious and wrote whatever came out of my pen and onto the paper. Eventually, after years of scribbling and publishing, my mother came back to me, not as the picture-perfect 1950's "mom" but as the humanly flawed yet insightfully gifted woman she had been. The realities were that she hadn't been ideal; she had been, like me, depressed; she had been in a bad marriage she had helped make that way;

she had made mistakes just like my father and everybody else; and she had struggled with life's inflictions and exhilarations.

For over 40 years, I had hidden her memory beneath layers of fiction, idealization and depression. When once again made real, she could still teach. When once again made whole, I could still learn. To paraphrase that great old country music classic, thank God I'm a mamma's boy.

The Evening Breeze Caressed The Trees

Finally, I surrendered. Rather than laying down arms, I drove to one of those commercial mail box stores and shipped off a goldplated Selmer saxophone and a black, wood-grained LeBlanc clarinet to the music department of my college alma mater for a modest tax deduction. Rock and roll had won. I had lost.

In retrospect, my defeat was inevitable as long ago as 1955 when Bill Haley and the Comets appeared in a movie called *Blackboard Jungle* and shouted, "one two three o'clock, four o'clock rock, five six seven o'clock, eight o'clock rock . . . we're gonna rock . . . around . . . the clock tonight." I didn't realize it at the time, but those shouts spelled trouble.

Back then, I was a teenage musician and the self-appointed heir to such big band greats as Glenn Miller, Duke Ellington, Tommy Dorsey, Les Brown and Benny Goodman. Inspired by Jimmy Stewart in the 1953 movie, *The Glenn Miller Story*, my friends and I organized a seven-piece dance band called The Aristo-Katz, which consisted of three saxophones, trumpet, trombone, piano and drums and which specialized in uneven renditions of classics like "Take The 'A' Train," "Sentimental Journey," "String of Pearls" and "One O'clock Jump."

After the seven of us learned how to stay in tune most of the time and to maintain a beat that was usually danceable, we hired ourselves out for beery fraternity parties and formal high school proms. Business was good and there seemed to be real truth in the bland, 1950's-style statement on our business cards — "The Aristo-Katz, For The Music EVERYBODY Likes."

Ten dollars a night was big money for a teenager in those days, but, my reward was something more transcendent. Late in each dance when couples were tired, slow-shuffling and cheek-to-cheek, I would stand up behind the lighted bandstand, give a slow downbeat, calm the brass, and play the alto saxophone solo to "Tenderly," one of the Aristo-Katz' favorite numbers. With my saxophone pushed straight out in front of me, I loved blowing air into that golden, French-made instrument; gliding my fingers across the keys; undulating my jaw for a smooth vibrato; and projecting a cool, metallic wail into darkened gymnasiums crowned with sparkling, mirrored balls.

Since I knew "Tenderly" by heart, I could play my solo, look out at the crowd and see dancers whisper the lyrics into their partners' ears. "The evening breeze, caressed the trees, tenderly. The trembling trees, embraced the breeze, tenderly." It was sublime.

When "Shake, Rattle and Roll" became a hit in 1954, the Aristo-Katz simply ignored the noisy commotion. Later, when *Blackboard Jungle* came to the screen in 1955, we disdained the raw, driving rhythm; laughed at the blaring guitars; and ridiculed the musicians' raunchy body movements. Our smug prediction was that this cacophony would disappear into squalid venues where greasy misfits gathered on their motorcycles and where things happened that were not portrayed on TV's *Father Knows Best*.

But we were wrong. After Bill Haley came Elvis Presley, Buddy Holly, Chuck Berry, Little Richard, The Big Bopper and a mounting succession of hits, all with that same pounding beat. Out went saxophone sections, white dinner jackets, crew cuts and embracing couples. In came electric guitars, raised collars, glistening hair and suggestive gyration.

The Aristo-Katz countered by updating our repertoire with some current but drippy tunes like Johnny Mathis' "Chances Are" and Pat Boone's "April Love." But when we ignored demands for "A Whole Lot-a Shakin' Goin' On" and instead played "Smoke Gets in Your Eyes," the groans swelled and the dancers thinned.

Things did not improve when I went off to college and played with a nine-piece orchestra called Ziggy Ziglar and his Midwestern Melody Makers.

During weekend dates in small prairie towns, I tolerated occasional requests for "old time" polkas so that big-boned Norwegians could clomp all over the floor; however, I balked at demands for Chubby Checker so those same Norwegians could "twist again, the way we did last summer." Disgusted, I quit the Melody Makers; packed away my instruments; and fought back by switching off radios and acting culturally superior.

Suddenly, in 1967, I forgot about the coming Dark Ages of American music and started playing again, this time for serious stakes. The Vietnam War was on; my draft board was asking pointed questions; and there was an opening for a last-chair clarinetist in the Army National Guard band. Together with several other conscientious clarinetists, I applied for this musical refuge and then worked for days, practicing scales, de-rusting my technique and strengthening my embouchure — the position of the lips over the clarinet mouthpiece. The National Guard held the audition on a hot July night in a fluorescently lighted armory. Each would-be draft avoider sucked on clarinet reeds, doodled out warm-up notes and joked about how life and limb might depend upon our sight-reading skills.

When the band's warrant officer distributed the previously unseen sheets of music, I thumbed through the pages and, to my relief, saw John Philip Sousa's "Stars and Stripes Forever" that I had played hundreds of times in high school and "Grenada," a Latin piece with some tricky key signatures I had just practiced. So far so good.

But then I came to the last try-out number. There before me, with complicated, inky markings and impossibly fast runs, was a rock and roll medley arranged for marching band that included, to my astonishment, Bill Haley's "Rock Around The Clock." Chosen to go first, I played "Stars and Stripes Forever" and "Grenada" smoothly but then lurched and squeaked my way through "Rock Around the Clock," bringing winces to the warrant officer's face.

Later, while the National Guard Band marched to its rock and roll medley without me, I received a form letter from President Lyndon Johnson. In blunt language, the President ordered me to report for active duty at Fort Lewis, Washington, which back then was a famous jumping-off point for Vietnam. The score was rock and roll two, me zero.

Decades have passed since Chubby Checker put me out of the music business and Bill Haley got me drafted. And years have gone by since I shipped off my saxophone and clarinet for a tax deduction. Still, like so many others throughout history who have been defeated by the primitive forces of bad taste, my resistance has continued and, today, I make more big band music than ever before.

Several nights a week, I don a portable tape player. I walk outside in the dark; and, bringing police cars to a crawl and driving pedestrians to the other side of the street, I vigorously conduct everything from Count Basie's "April In Paris" to Stan Kenton's "Artistry In Rhythm." Sometimes, if the right tape is on, I'll give a slow downbeat, calm the brass and, after a few bars, cue the solo in "Tenderly."

When the alto saxophone begins to wail, I just know that, someday, mirrored balls will once more rotate and slow-dancing couples will again whisper those evocative lyrics into each others' ears. "Then you and I, came wandering by, and lost in a sigh were we . . . ."

CHAPTER TWO

MY FATHER

HIS WARS WITH THE JAPANESE, PTSD, ALZHEIMER'S AND ME

Letters From Hell

Christmas 1960

December Thaw

His Last Memory

Could I Euthanize My Father?

Letters From Hell

In bold print, the cover sheet read, "A Young Doctor Goes to War-Capt. T.D. Baird, M.D., South Pacific, September-October, 1944." Attached were twenty-six letters in chronological order, neatly typed transcriptions from the original WWII "V-Mail." I was stunned.

"Capt. T.D. Baird, M.D." was my father and these were letters he had written more than sixty years ago — letters I knew nothing about. They were sent to me by my 97-year-old uncle and, to my profound regret, they arrived after I had published a novel based loosely on my father's life.

Specifically, my novel, *Beyond Peleliu*, was about an Army doctor who, just like my father, had been inexplicably wounded during the WWII Battle of Peleliu and whose wound, just like my father's, had traumatized him as well as his wife, son, and, eventually, grandchildren. The novel was my way of expressing in fiction what I did not know in fact and what I had spent decades yearning to know to the point of obsession: How had my father been wounded in the Battle of Peleliu?

What I did know was that he had been a U.S. Army surgeon in the 81st "Wildcat" Division which, on September 17, 1944, invaded the Island of Angaur. During that battle, my father and his fellow medical corpsmen had to cope with 1,614 American casualties. Later, on October 15, the 81st Division relieved the First Marine Division on the nearby Island of Peleliu where there had already been 6,786 Marine casualties and where there would be another 1,601 Army casualties. On both islands, the Japanese fought from dense jungles and unseen caves and tunnels and the fighting was fierce.

It was during the Battle of Peleliu that my father had somehow been wounded in the left hand. Although there were conflicting stories about how it had happened, there was no doubt that he had come home with three permanently splinted fingers, diminished surgical skills and an un-diagnosed case of "PTSD" or Post Traumatic Stress Disorder. His PTSD symptoms-depression, alcoholism, anger and domestic violence-were demons that drove him to fly into harangues, administer blistering spankings and conduct dinner table quizzes in which wrong answers were punishable by push-ups, sometimes as many as a hundred.

My mother excused his behavior, explaining that the "war had changed him" and implying that the war was to blame, not him. My mother theo-rized that he had killed a Japanese soldier with his bare hands; he was in field surgery for over eighty straight hours without sleep; and then, in the tropical heat and madness of combat, he had become delirious and shot himself. As a boy, I dimly recall seeing a document that may have supported her theory but that was almost 50 years ago and, today, my memory is as vague as it is suspect.

Yet, if she was right, why had he said that a "Jap sniper" had shot him? Why had he also claimed that "a Jeep door" had slammed against his left hand? After years of wrestling with his inconsistencies and my own ob-session, I decided to make up my own story about Peleliu, the wound and its generational impact. Thus the novel.

As I stared at the stack of letters, it struck me that they might hold the answer. Maybe my father had written about the wound in these letters and that was an intriguing thought. If I finally learned the truth, then I could write a sequel or, better yet, a non-fiction account about what had actually happened on Peleliu and what the aftermath had actually been for our family. Enthralled by this new literary prospect, I started having conversations in my head with my agent about a work of non-fiction, pos-sible titles and another royalty stream. As an added bonus, the second book could promote the first.

Excited, I riffled through the letters and, ignoring their contents, focused on dates. Since the 81st Division had landed on Peleliu on October 15, the letters from that date forward would hold the key. When I reached October, I stopped riffling and proceeded slowly, page by page, until I came to the letter dated October 14, 1944. Taking a deep breath, I turned past it and found nothing, except five blank pages. The letters were all from Angaur, none was from Peleliu.

It didn't take long for the realities to sink in. There wasn't going to be a new book, a happy agent, more royalties, a plug for Beyond Peleliu or another literary credit for me to crow about. None of that was going to happen and, of course, I would never know the truth about Peleliu and my father's wound. Frustrated and disappointed, I tossed the letters aside and began to feel sorry for myself. That is, until a tsunami of shame hit me.

I hadn't bothered to read the letters from Angaur and Angaur might have had as much to do with his PTSD as Peleliu. Moreover, I had been indifferent to the possibility that the Battle of Peleliu may have been so ghastly and the wound so traumatic that he may never have wanted to write, or even tell the truth, about what had happened. Indeed, it never occurred to me that he may have wanted his secret to remain a secret, especially if my mother's theory was correct.

My thoughts had not been about him, his wishes or the hell he must have gone through while in mortal combat. Instead, I had rushed into a blindly concocted pipedream about books, agents, royalties, and literary credits. In my self-absorption, all I had thought about was myself. What kind of a son was that?

With the answer to that question searing my conscience, I sat down and started to slowly pore over his letters from Angaur. What I read made me proud of him and feel worse about myself.

In his letters to "Mrs. Holmes," which was his code word for my mother, he wrote: "all surgery is done under fire and in field conditions;" "they got the Jap gunner who tried to shoot me yesterday;" "the Japs do not give up, they are fanatics;" "this is a holocaust;" "under fire continually day and night;" "another night of flares and grenades;" "did 4 amputations yesterday;" "broke down twice;" "six inches of rain in 30 minutes;" "I sleep in my foxhole with my .45 loaded and cocked;" "temp. over 100 and endless rain and mud;" "been shot at so many times by snipers that I don't even bother to duck anymore;" "more trauma surgery than I ever expected to do in my whole life;" "the Japs hit us by air last night;" "I've awarded six Purple Hearts;" "machine gun bullets bounced all around me;" "land crabs, mosquitoes, flies and vermin;" "must write sympathy letters;" and, in the middle of battle, he "delivered a baby from a young Korean woman."

He also wrote about me, then three years old: "you can tell Petey that there are real, wild monkeys on this island as well as snakes;" "you can tell Peter boy that there is a train here and I'll draw a picture of it for him;" "I keep wondering what you and Peter are doing;" and "by all means see that Peter has a Christmas tree and take a picture and send it to me."

As I put the letters down, Peleliu didn't matter anymore but my father did, now more than ever. Finally, I am beyond Peleliu.

Christmas 1960

Within minutes of picking me up at the Spokane railroad station where I had just arrived on the train for Christmas break from college, my father started laying down some new rules.

"I don't want any holiday decorations or festivities at the house," he announced as we drove through intermittent snow flurries on our way home. He went on: "All that fa-la-la-la-la stuff died with your mother. I don't want to even think about it this year. Do you understand?"

My response was a cross between the affirmative "uh-huh" and the negative "uh-uh" but the ambiguity was lost on my father, who already had started to bait me about how bad John F. Kennedy was going to be for the country and how the president-elect would immediately "social-ize" medicine, including my doctor father. As the car skidded on some black ice and we almost went into the ditch, I put off defending Kennedy's social agenda but resented my father's ban on Christmas.

Although our family struggled throughout each year with episodes of depression, alcoholism and aggression, we typically coalesced at Christmas when an unspoken truce took effect. My parents genuinely seemed to like each other in late December and, even more astonishing, my father and I could talk rationally about our differences over politics, civil rights and the arms race. Indeed, the three of us had never been closer than we were a year earlier when my cancer-stricken mother celebrated her last Christmas.

By the time we pulled into our driveway, it was late and the snow had drifted up to block the garage. After helping with the bags, my father bade me good night with a gruff order: "Tomorrow, shovel the snow from the porch, walks and driveway." Then he added, "I have surgery almost all day, so I'll pick you up around 5:30 or 6:00 and we'll go out for dinner."

Late the next afternoon after a full day at the hospital, he walked into the living room and started to complain about my snow-shoveling performance. Stopping abruptly in mid-sentence, he paused for a second and then barked, "What is that thing?"

It was a puny, three-foot-tall, sparsely branched evergreen that I had bought earlier in the day and had decorated with some strands of tinsel, a few bulbs and a half-string of lights. Standing bent over in the living room, where my mother traditionally put our resplendent trees, this pathetic little fir tree looked like something out of a cartoon.

"It's a Christmas tree," I answered, irritated. "Mom would have wanted us to celebrate the holidays this year and do the best we could under the circumstances."

Although I'd been an all-star football player in high school, I was no match for my much larger, World War II combat veteran father who always had the advantage of limitless rage. In seconds, the tree, lights, ornaments and I were tangled up in the very snowbank that I had just shoveled up outside our front door, which my father then slammed shut and dead-bolted from the inside.

Later, on Christmas Eve afternoon, word reached me at a neighbor's house where I had taken refuge. According to the message, my father was chagrined about "our" blow-up but still adamantly opposed any Christmas in our home. While he wanted me back, his most urgent request was to join him as a "buffer" that evening for a Christmas Eve midnight Mass. Evidently, the woman he was dating, a devout Episcopalian, was holding him to a loose promise that he had made weeks earlier and was dragging him to this high Mass.

Quite apart from our fracas over the tree, I could not believe that either one of us belonged in church at any time, let alone on Christmas Eve. After all, my impatient father detested liturgical pomp, and the only vestiges of our Scottish Presbyterian heritage were my guilt and his revulsion for

Catholicism. Nevertheless, after some aggressive lobbying by mutual friends, I reluctantly agreed to see if an Anglican God could bring us together, at least for Christmas Eve.

From my father's perspective, this high midnight Mass — with its priests, wine, wafers, choir, brass band, pennants, acolytes and interminable homily — could just as well have taken place at Vatican City. For him, it was torture. He squirmed, cursed under his breath and awkwardly moved sideways to let believers in and out of the pew for communion. Indeed, as the night deepened and the service dragged on, even the faithful started to fidget, check watches and wonder in low tones if they would ever get home in time to assemble the toys before dawn.

Finally, after a seeming eternity, the procession trooped back down the aisle toward the main entrance, singing what was billed as the closing anthem. But then, all of them — priests, choir, band, standard-bearers and acolytes — collectively pivoted, faced the altar and took several paces forward, threatening to return for another ecclesiastical round.

Confronted with the unendurable, my agitated father could not contain himself. In one of those acoustically perfect moments when there was total silence and even the slightest sound could have filled the sanctuary, my father erupted with, "Oh, Jesus Christ don't go back."

At once, more than 300 worshipers released their accumulated tensions, burst into laughter and drowned out the benediction from a surprised and rattled priest. Only a piercing organ postlude restored any religious solemnity to the occasion, as liberated Christians rose to their feet, surged toward the exits and turned — smiling, waving and pointing — in the direction of my father.

After dropping off his furious Episcopalian date, my father and I drove home without having exchanged more than a few perfunctory words all night. Once inside the house and seated across from each other in our semi-darkened living room, I broke the virtual silence.

"I must have inherited your revulsion for liturgy, Dad, because I thought you were just great in church tonight."

He frowned, thought for a moment, then asked, "Is that tree still around here somewhere?"

Not knowing whether I should brace myself for another explosion or try to remind him of our traditional holiday truce, I was tentative in answering his question.

"Well . . . if I recall correctly . . . I think it's probably next door . . . leaning against the Nelson's house," I said.

"Tell you what," he proposed, without softening his tone or breaking a smile. "I'll make us the two stiffest Christmas Eve drinks ever mixed. You go out, get that tree and bring it in here."

Rising out of his chair, he looked at a spot in front of the large picture window that overlooked the snow-covered wheat fields just outside town. "You put that little guy right there," he directed, pointing. "That's exactly where your mother would have wanted it to go."

December Thaw

The sound of the twin turboprop engines dropped an octave and the eighteen-seat Jetstream nosed downward, through a winter cloud layer and toward a rural airport in northern Idaho. When the Snake River became dimly visible in the gray, December overcast, I took her letter out for a last read.

"You will notice some major changes in your father," his wife had written. "Although he is very excited about seeing you after all these years, please understand that he gets confused and frustrated these days." She added, "Plan to spend the night with us and we will pick you up at the airport."

My father and I had not seen each other in nearly fifteen years. United biologically by a wife and mother who had died thirty years ago and joined historically by a past that was often boozy and violent, he and I had gone through one battle after another over the years until we finally parted with such fury and hurt that the break seemed irreparable.

Yet, there I was, walking across a snow-specked tarmac, looking for him through the windows of the small, glassed-in reception area and wondering what he would look like and what the protocol should be after years of strained silence. A handshake? A hug? What about, "How've you been?" Never, even in the best of times, had we ever said anything to each other resembling, "I love you."

Once inside the gate, I saw him. Always a big man who carried his heft as if he were well-exercised and who projected an intimidating confidence through a powerful and resonant voice, he was now strikingly different. At eighty-one, he had lost height, gained girth and become an untoned slab of tired flesh. After bringing me gradually into focus, he moved stiffly with a cane in my direction and, swallowing the back half of each word, said something that I did not understand.

Once at close range, he resolved the protocol issue, extended his right hand as far as his arm would take it and put on that disapproving expression always reserved for his only child. Shaking his hand, I mumbled something that had the word "sir" in it and wondered whether we were about to climb back into the ring for another round of father against son or, from his perspective, son against father.

In retrospect, our incompatibility was probably inevitable. He was born into poverty, deprived of a mother by a doctor's clumsy overdose of chloroform, delayed from reaching medical school by the Depression, drafted into World War Two during the early days of his marriage, and shot in his surgeon's hand while with the Army in the South Pacific. Once discharged from the Army, he confronted exclusionary bonds forged between mother and son during the War and became a workaholic physician who suffered from periodic bouts of untreated alcoholism, depression and aggression and who could never really accept his son. Eventually, his disapproval culminated during the Vietnam War when he lobbied the local Selective Service Board to have me drafted and, as he saw it, fight for freedom the way he had.

After our awkward encounter inside the terminal building, we loaded his arthritic weight into the passenger's side of the front seat, drove to their home overlooking the Snake River and settled in for an apprehensive afternoon and evening. As we diplomatically made our way through some stiff drinks and a late lunch and the exchanged small talk about the darkening clouds over the river, it slowly became apparent that a change was in progress and that, at least for now, there would be no more battles, rages or hurt.

At the same time, something about my father was wrong, off-centered, even crazy. Time after time, he slipped off the rational track, losing the conversation and sometimes confusing me for a deceased surgeon he had scrubbed with often in the past. He could not find the mustard jar that was right in front of him. When he raised his drink glass, I saw that he wore two wristwatches. After calling his wife of twenty-five years by my mother's name and then realizing the mistake, he loudly promised that, crippled and confined at age eighty-one, he would never "step out" or cheat on her. While wobbling on a treadmill for three minutes to elevate his pulse, he breathlessly estimated that his distance was "between nine and ten miles"; and then, though barely able to get in and out of the shower, he looked out at the powerful Snake River and confidently said he could swim it. In the men's room of a nearby country club where we went for an early dinner, he turned away from the urinal and, while still unzipped and conspicuous, attempted to introduce me to a startled stranger who had just walked through the door.

"The doctors are hedging," his wife explained when he was out of the room, "but they believe that your dad probably has Alzheimer's disease. The last time your father was examined, he told the doctor that Harry Truman was President. Unfortunately, he refuses to go to any major medical center for further evaluation and he erupts with anger whenever we press the issue." She went on to elaborate that the condition had been getting progressively worse for about two years and that, in addition to the mental disorientation, the disease had caused incontinence, rage and almost total dependence. Increasingly, his wife was a victim too because, fifteen years younger than he and still active, she was forced into house-bound seclusion as a round-the-clock nurse and housekeeper.

Yet, whatever was disrupting his neuro-synapses was also generating an unprecedented flow of paternal behavior. He asked about the ten-year old granddaughter he had never seen and about the college student grandsons he had last seen when they were in preschool. Though he could not keep the two grandsons straight, he pored over the photographs I brought, enthralled. He genuinely wanted to know about me, my work, my marriage, my problems and my life. Indeed, as the afternoon wore on, he actually ministered to me in some touching but bewildering ways: bringing me oversized clothes and slippers that I could not wear; pouring me a new drink when I already had a fresh one; writing out unintelligible prescriptions for maladies that I didn't have; and appearing naked, with a pill in one hand and a glass of water in the other, offering immediate treatment for a non-existent peptic ulcer.

Outside, the December darkness fell early as it does at that latitude and, from the arc lights on the grain elevators across the Snake, we could make out a few windless snowflakes and some patchy reflections on the river. As time passed, our conversation ebbed into a long silence while my father stared out the window at the headlights of a freight train on the opposite shore. Slowly, he turned to me and, with an expression that I had never seen before but that I later took to be love, said "I know-that I wasn't much of a father to you, Pete, and that I made a lot of mistakes. I want you to know that I am very sorry."

Astonished and moved by the warmth of this December thaw from an implacable man whom I had fought all my life for approval, all I could think to say was, "That's alright, Dad. It really is okay." And it was, finally.

His Last Memory

Ignoring travel advisories from the Idaho Highway Patrol, the airport limo driver downshifted and then eased the van into the snow-packed curves. "Mister, you're awful lucky that I'd drive the Lewiston grade on a day like this," he said over the whine from low gear. After the van fishtailed on some ice and grazed the guardrail, he grumbled, "Must be damned important for you to reach Moscow today." It was.

My father was there in a nursing home, suffering from Alzheimer's disease. Before he surrendered the last neurosynapse of lucidity, I had to talk with him, not about "How are you feeling?" or "Are they treating you alright here?", but about some personal debris from the 1950's that still smoldered like radioactive waste.

Once before we had talked of such things. It happened last December, when the disease had softened his resentments, ended decades of conflict between us and actually brought us together. Meeting for the first time in fifteen years, we worked around his occasional confusion and spoke in the abstract about mistakes and hurts and, by nightfall, even about apology and forgiveness. There had been a transformation, though much was left for later.

Now, a year had passed and we needed to finish our conversation, if that was medically possible. His wife had explained the problems on the telephone: "Your father cries; he has lost weight; his incontinence is worse; and the scans show that his brain is actually shrinking." She went on: "He still has some memory and conversational capacity, but they are affected by the tranquilizers he takes for the violence."

Like a bad boy, my 82-year-old father had been expelled from four different rest homes for having thrashed patients and staff members over

a missing baseball hat, the tardiness of a non-existent band and an assort-
ment of homophobic fictions. Sadly, his violence had preceded the
Alzheimer's by a lifetime. Learned from his own father, reinforced on the
streets where he was a motherless kid and then validated in World War Two
combat, his violence was something I still remembered forty years later,
whether awake or asleep. We needed to talk about it, finally.

Once in town, I paid the driver, rented a car and set out through the snow-
storm to find the nursing home. Recognizing the downtown intersection
where a holiday banner once read, "Put Christ Back Into Christmas — The
Moscow Chamber of Commerce," I found my bearings and then drove
past the hospital where my father had been a prominent physician and
where, thirty years ago, he had sobbed to my comatose mother about the
same things he and I needed to resolve. The nursing home was beyond
the hospital, on a hill overlooking the city.

Unlocking the double doors to the Alzheimer's unit, the nursing home
director jerked his tie up into a simulated hangman's noose as he described
how my father almost strangled him. Beyond the double doors, a wide
corridor led to a multipurpose room where Alzheimer's patients lived out
their daytime degenerations, staring at the floor, wandering about or making
noises with the English language.

He was seated against the wall, with an outdated *The American Medical
Association Journal* in his lap. Eighty pounds gone, eyes leadened and skin
charcoaled, he looked like a voodoo doll of his former self. After some
coaching, he said my name, stood up into a hunch and greeted me formally as he always did, with a handshake at the end of a fully extended
arm. During some small talk that was surprisingly rational, he shuffled
me off to his private room and threw hostile glances back at the stares
that followed us.

Encouraged by the coherence of our conversation, I asked about the
scenes from the 1950's that still scripted my nightmares and drove my depression. "Dad, do you remember the day that you were drunk and took

out your .38 revolver and waved it around at Mom and me?" Silence. "Were you really going to kill us?" No response. "When I got horribly sick and couldn't walk, why did you accuse me of malingering, leave the house and force Mom to get another doctor to diagnose the polio?" Nothing. "Did Mom ever forgive you for the violence?" Blank stare.

Then suddenly, he reacted all at once, with sheets of tears, gestures of remonstration and blubbery sounds intended to be words. As I watched this sick and dying man weep and struggle to say something, the shameful truth finally registered that I was not here for him or his comfort but for me, my nightmares and my depression. Like a bad cop, I had come to wring confessions out of someone with half his brain gone and then, in the name of closure, settle old scores by dispensing morally superior forgiveness. It was disgusting.

For what seemed like a long time, we just stared at each other through our tears and shame until I remembered the photographs in my briefcase. Though they were no more than fascinating strangers to him, the faces of his grandchildren ended the tears and inspired rapt attention. Looking next at a photograph of my wife and me, he wanted to know which one was my wife. He could not place my mother, despite twenty years of marriage to her. Yet, he quickly connected the gaunt, unsmiling face from the late 1940's with his own dyspeptic father.

The last photograph, a faded oval in a small antique frame, pictured a soft-featured, faintly smiling young woman who wore a white lace dress with a high collar and who had her hair done up in a Gibson Girl style. "LaRoux," he said without hesitation, "that's-my-mother." She had died in 1914 from an inept doctor's overdose of chloroform. My father was six at the time. Repeating her name with a long, slow "oo" sound, he took her photograph gently in both hands, staring. When I asked how he could recognize that face after seventy-six years, he simply said, "LaRoux-I'll-remember."

Again and again, we pored over the photographs. Each time his reactions were the same. Each time he responded as if he had never seen the images before. Through the day, we took breaks and I helped him eat, go to the bathroom, and find things he needed. Afterwards, we returned to the photographs and especially to LaRoux, whose face he would study for long stretches and whose name he repeated with that evocative "oo" sound.

At day's end, he shuffled with me to the locked double doors and extended his right arm its entire length for our farewell handshake. Through the doors' wire-meshed windows, he watched and cried as I walked to the reception area and then left his sight for the parking lot. Outside, the storm had passed and the snow was already melting.

Alzheimer's had brought us together again. There were no confessions, no delayed redress disguised as forgiveness. Instead, for the first time, I actually took care of my father: cutting his food, taking him to the bathroom and, most important, showing him the face of a white-laced young woman who gently smiled at him from before 1914 and beyond his tomorrows.

"LaRoux," he had said, "I'll remember."

Could I Euthanize My Father?

The last time I saw my frail, 91-year-old father was in August, 2000 in the empty snack bar of the State Veterans Home in Lewiston, Idaho. He was slumped over in a wheelchair, head listing to one side and mouth wheezing spent air. Around him on the walls were World War Two photographs of the Veterans Home's residents when they were B-29 pilots, tank commanders, naval gunners and, in my father's case, an army surgeon.

Seated next to me in the snack bar was my stepmother who had been forced, years earlier, to divorce my father to preserve their medically depleted assets. "He's lost ground since the last time you were here," she said. "I'm not sure he even recognizes me anymore. In fact, the only thing I am sure of is that he'll open his mouth at the mention of ice cream."

For over ten years, Alzheimer's had been wasting my father's brain and body. Although once a booming-voiced, 6 feet, 2 inch physician who had fought orphanhood, poverty and the Japanese Army in the South Pacific, he was now a shrunken voodoo doll of his former self. Despite his steep decline, his autonomic nervous system had kept on working and, without respiration or medication, his heart, kidneys, and digestive organs had continued to function. All he had needed for organic continuation was the food, drink, shelter and kindness at the Veterans Home where they affectionately called him "Doc."

Because he was helpless, hopeless and worst of all mindless, my father was not alive in any meaningful sense. Nor would he ever be again. On the other hand, he wasn't dead yet and he wasn't dying either. For want of a better word, he was "un-dead" and he would have hated it.

In the 1940's and 1950's when I was growing up, he had repeatedly denounced geriatric care centers as "vegetable farms" and had made me swear that he would never get "planted" in one. Every time the subject of his own possible incapacity came up, he would launch into a lecture about the advantages real vegetables had over the human variety because "turnips and carrots don't stare at the floor, they don't drool down their chins and they don't pee or poop in their pants."

Although he opposed abortion, my father embraced euthanasia. To him, these views were not contradictory and were based upon the simple concept that, once begun, life should proceed and, once over, life should end. "You don't see any addled or decrepit rabbits, birds or deer hanging around, do you?," he would ask rhetorically.

Given that basic philosophy, my father never performed an abortion in his life but he did help countless patients escape their incurable sufferings. As a field surgeon during the World War Two battles of Angaur and Peleliu, he never hesitated to give hopelessly wounded soldiers lethal blasts of morphine. As a country doctor in northern Idaho, he routinely did for families and their stricken loved ones the same thing he had done for my own comatose, cancer-afflicted mother.

Rising from her chair in the snack bar, my stepmother placed a hand on my father's shoulder and gently roused him. Abruptly, he stopped snoring, opened his eyes and looked up at her with a seemingly intelligent gaze. While stroking the back of his head, she said, "Every day someone reads the newspaper to him and I stop by several times a week and talk to him about golf and the weather and the comings and goings of our friends, don't I honey?" He responded with a faint smile.

Since he had not yet acknowledged my presence, she leaned over and, in a louder voice, said, "Tom, Peter is here. You remember Peter, don't you? Peter is your son and he has come all the way from Phoenix to visit you again. Isn't that nice?" After several more promptings, he mimicked what she had said and slurred out the word, "P-e-e-e-t-er." Then he struggled to say something else but could not and broke down into a tearless cry.

"I'm going down the hall and talk to the nurses about next week's schedule," my stepmother said. "I'll let you guys catch up on each other." For a few long moments after she left, my father and I stared at each other like stupefied strangers.

Eventually, I broke the silence with a stream of newsy small talk. Touched and encouraged by his saying "P-e-e-e-t-er," I rattled on in unnecessary detail about his brothers, grandchildren and great grandchildren and also about my mother whose death my father had compassionately precipitated. In the remote chance he was lucid, I also ignored our political differences and tried to cheer him up by lying and telling him that President Clinton had been impeached.

About the time I ran out of newsy chit-chat, he dozed off and started listing, wheezing and snoring again. As I always did on these occasions, I felt guilty because of my broken promises and I also felt conflicted because I never knew what to do. Should I find a pillow and asphyxiate him? Cajole a doctor into giving him an overdose of morphine? Bribe the staff into starving and dehydrating him? Get myself named as his guardian and ask for judicial permission to terminate his life in the most humane manner possible?

Put more bluntly, did I have the guts to kill my own father? Could I actually go down the hall, find a pillow and come back and press it against his face for five or ten minutes? If so, his life would be mercifully over but mine could become seriously complicated.

As a lawyer, I knew that every state, including Idaho, makes it a crime to deliberately take the life of another human being. There aren't any exceptions for good intentions or merciful endings. It is called homicide and it is and ought to be serious business. Although prosecutors are usually reluctant to indict in mercy killing cases and juries are even more reluctant to convict, I had no guaranty of immunity and I was very much aware that spouses, children and physicians had been convicted in other states and had been sent to prison for their acts of euthanasia.

Before flying to Idaho, I had done some legal research and had studied the U.S. Supreme Court's decision in *Cruzan v. Director*, which said that, ". . . we assume that the United States Constitution would grant a competent person a constitutionally protected right to refuse lifesaving hydration and nutrition." 497 U.S. 261, 110 S.Ct. 2841 (1990). However, that case was of no help to me because, to exercise that right, my father had to be competent and he wasn't, at all. Making matters worse, he had not spelled out his wishes in a living will or in an advance health care directive which would not be a defense to an Idaho murder charge but which might discourage a prosecutor or a grand jury from indicting me.

I had also read the famous case *In Re Quinlan*, 70 N.J. 10, 355 A.2d 647 (1976), *cert denied* 429 U.S.922 (1976), from New Jersey where the court had appointed the comatose daughter's father as her legal guardian and then authorized him to "pull the plug" by switching off her respirator. But my father was not on any life support and there wasn't any medical device to "unplug."

Complicating matters even more, I had not lived in Idaho for over 40 years and did not know any doctor who would, as my father once did, discreetly arrange for a painless starvation, dehydration or overdose. If I had to do the dirty work myself, then I confronted the U.S. Supreme Court's 1997 decisions in *Washington v. Glucksberg*, 117 S. Ct. 2258 (1997), and *Vacco v. Quill*, 117 S. Ct. 2293 (1997), which, while holding it was lawful to withdraw medical life support and permit the underlying disease to kill the patient, said that a state could make it a crime for someone like me to be the cause of death by, for example, asphyxiating my father.

For almost an hour, I sat and studied my wheezing, snoring father and despaired my broken promises, his pathetic condition and our difficult options. Eventually, I did as I always had done and played it safe, let the disease have its way with him and avoided the risks of being convicted of a crime in Idaho and losing my license to practice law in Arizona. Of all the tears one can shed, I suspect those from shame are the worst.

In time, my stepmother returned to the snack bar to take me to the airport and I kissed my father goodbye for what would be the last time. As the twin turboprop Jetstream gained altitude from the Lewiston-Clarkston Airport and the Snake River separating Idaho and Washington became an ever-narrowing ribbon, I still felt bad but took some comfort in knowing that, if I ever became un-dead, my family would not be legally precluded from doing what I wanted done.

By the year 2020, I will be the same age my father was when Alzheimer's first attacked his competence and continence and I know very well that Alzheimer's can be hereditary and that there is no cure in sight. Fortunately, by 2020, virtually every state in the country will respect a patient's explicit wishes if those instructions are spelled out in a written, signed advance health care directive.

While some states already allow health care workers to withhold food and fluids while other states do not, the march is on toward honoring patient instructions. In varying forms and degrees, this trend is apparent in Arizona, other states, and the Draft Uniform Rights of the Terminally Ill Act. See, Collin, *Durable Powers of Attorney And Health Care Directives* (Clark Boardman Callaghan, 3rd ed., 1994).

In Oregon, voters even enacted a referendum that allows physicians to lawfully assist in a patient's suicide. However, in 2002, Attorney General John Ashcroft attempted, unsuccessfully, to invalidate that law in *Oregon v. Ashcroft*, 192 F. Supp. 2d 1077 (D. Ore, 2002). See "Physician-Assisted Suicide Law Stands, Judge Strikes Down Ashcroft Directive Nullifying Oregon Law," 1 No. 15 A.B.A. J.E-Report 1, 1 (2002).

If my vision for 2020 turns out to be 20/20 and if I am un-dead by that time, all my family will have to do is give my advance directive to the health care people in charge and they will have the legal authority to honor most, if not all, of my specified desires. Neither my wife nor my children will have to torture their souls, as I did for so many years, about possibly bumping me off themselves. And that turns out to be vastly more important than I had ever imagined.

Several months later, my father suffered a massive stroke and died peacefully. Although I still believe that his life was over and should have ended ten years ago, I am surprisingly relieved that the cause of death was "Alzheimer's" and not "asphyxiation."

CHAPTER THREE

FAMILY MAN
WIVES, KIDS, COPS, AND SEX VIDEOS

Snoring Through Two Marriages

Magic And Herpes In Las Vegas

Moving Out

My Son The Lawyer

The Night The Police Came

Watching Sex Videos With My Wife

Snoring Through Two Marriages

Since I was always asleep whenever the ruckus allegedly rattled teeth and rocked beds, I never thought my snoring — uncharitably called "honking" — or my tossing and turnings — dubbed "thrashings" — could be as bad as a light-sleeping first wife and an even lighter-sleeping second wife had claimed. Was it my fault that they each went bug-eyed at the tug of a pillow or the flush of a toilet?

To be nice, I kept my doubts to myself and made all the right noises about sympathy and helplessness. In addition, I tolerated separate mattresses; elbows in my ribs; different bedrooms; plugs in their ears; middle-of-the-night cries to "turn over on your side;" a plastic clip in my nose; and a bed-side machine that blared out ersatz sounds of rain, surf, crickets, foghorns and loons. There was even an electronic wrist gizmo I wore that was supposed to buzz, vibrate and wake me up whenever I snored but it never worked because the buzzing and vibrating went on all night.

Recently, in my mid-fifties, I started having difficulty sleeping, getting up in the morning, and staying alert. At night, I would wake up choking for air, finding bedcovers kicked off onto the floor, and needing to visit the bathroom. During the day, I was an irritable zombie who required naps for energy and aspirin for headaches. Something was wrong.

"You probably have obstructive sleep apnea," the pulmonary specialist explained. "That means your airway closes when you are asleep; you are momentarily deprived of oxygen; you gasp and writhe for breath; you wake up, often without realizing it; and you don't reach the deepest and most important sleep stages, especially the REM or Rapid Eye Movement phase." He ended our session by scheduling me for an overnight stay in the sleep clinic where I would be "wired up."

As it turned out, "wired up" was an understatement. After I entered the clinic at 9:30 p.m., a chatty technician taped wires to my scalp, forehead, nose, throat, chest, abdomen, and legs. The wires ran into wall jacks which, she explained, would transmit data to a control room where she would be listening to sounds from my throat microphone and where she would be watching me through an infrared, closed-circuit television system.

Once I was tethered and tucked in, she wanted to know if I had any questions. Secretly, I wondered what the data would show if I experienced a nocturnal stiffening in my nether region but, because that hadn't happened in a long time, I contained my curiosity. However, I did ask how I was going to make my nightly pilgrimages to the bathroom without tripping over wires or getting electrocuted.

"That's a common question," she laughed. "Just say something, I'll hear it on the throat mike and come in and help." For the next eight hours whenever I self-consciously mumbled "gotta go," she would appear, turn on the light, unplug the wires, drape them in my arms, and warn me about loose ends getting flushed down the roaring, industrial toilet.

Two weeks later, I received a "Polysomnography Report" that reflected what my wives had carped about — "loud snoring noted" and "increased motor movement detected" — and that also confirmed what the doctor had suspected — "obstructive sleep apnea." When I read in the report that there had been eleven "spontaneous arousals per hour," my libido was suddenly born again until I realized that, in this context, "arousal" meant sleep disturbance.

In my follow-up session, the doctor explained that my options were to "lose 60 pounds" and I haven't lost one pound in ten years of trying; "take medication" and I already swallow six pills a day for such in-style afflictions as high cholesterol and depression; "have surgery" and I can't tolerate the pain of a mild sore throat; or "use a CPAP," which stands for "Continual Positive Air Pressure." The choice was easy.

Now when I retire, I don a nose mask that is held in place by four straps from an oddly shaped, white skull cap. The nose mask is, in turn, connected to a five-foot hose that runs to a CPAP pump that generates pressure that acts as an "air-splint" that holds my breathing passage open. Once everything is plugged in and strapped on, I look like a frogman wearing a jockstrap over my head and sounding like Darth Vader whenever my mouth opens and pressurized air hisses out.

The CPAP is cumbersome and it took some getting used to but it works. Gone is the apnea and gone too are the thrashings, snoring, choking, headaches, daytime drowsiness, and spousal grumblings. Perhaps because I'm sleeping more soundly, my bathroom pilgrimages are now only occasional and, sometimes, I even wake up with one of those stiffenings which, according to the literature, are caused by testosterone releases that occur during REM sleep and that I probably had been missing out on for years.

These days, I'm well-rested but, nevertheless, ethically troubled that I may owe my ex-wife and my current wife apologies for having deprived them of years of sleep and, especially, for having dismissed their complaints as exaggerated carpings. After all, the tests did prove that I have a sleep disorder and, therefore, they might have been heavier sleepers than I had ever thought. On the other hand, I didn't notice any symptoms until a short time ago and they couldn't have been deep sleepers because of their cat-like reactions to tugged pillows and flushed toilets.

Obviously, I'll have to sleep on the apology.

Magic And Herpes In Las Vegas

From behind the brass and darkly marbled front desk of Caesar's Palace in Las Vegas, the clerk welcomed me and talked about oversized jackpots as he took a credit card imprint and did some hunting and pecking on a computer keyboard. After the registration ritual was over, he waved to a bellman, put the room keys on the counter and, in a guy-to-guy tone, said, "As requested, you'll be staying in Fantasy Tower and I'm sure that you and your 'wife' will have lots of fun up there."

In point of fact, I had not made the reservations; I had never heard of Fantasy Tower; and the scowling, conservatively-attired woman standing 10 feet behind me was my wife, not my "wife." Attractive, Stanford-educated and a serious student of religion, she was progressively hating every minute in Las Vegas more than the one before. Indeed, everything within range of her radar-like glare — hundreds of cranking, tinkling slot machines; mini-skirted cocktail waitresses lightly clad as Roman slaves; and men wearing gold chains and chest hair instead of shirts — had my fault written all over it.

I had traveled to Las Vegas, dragging her with me, to give an after-dinner magic show for a group of shopping center conventioneers who had made our reservations at Caesar's Palace and who, as they explained later, had thought that we would "get a kick" out of Fantasy Tower. Although I am a partner in a large Phoenix law firm, magic has been my life-long passion and, for almost 20 years, I have been giving a pseudo mind-reading act around the country for groups that, in return for my conjuring services, will donate money to cancer research.

But not even the conventioneers' promise of a $7,500 gift to the American Cancer Society was enough to contain my wife's revulsion or to put me at ease. When the bellman reacted to the words "Fantasy Tower" with a wide grin, I squirmed and she started muttering lines from *Genesis* about "Sodom and Gomorrah."

After an elevator ride with some gamblers who stank of too much alcohol at 2:30 in the afternoon, the bellman parked our bags in the room; he huffed off because I hadn't slipped him a fat enough wad of bills; and we were left alone to gape at our Fantasy Tower accommodations. The first thing we noticed was that virtually everything — the deep pile carpet, flocked wallpaper, heavy drapes, upholstery, bedspreads and lampshades — was a deep, hemoglobin red.

Then there was the immense, canopied bed which occupied the room like an aircraft carrier in dry dock. While its size suggested a certain thematic centrality, the bed itself was not half as interesting as the overhead ceiling mirror.

For a long minute, we stared at the reflected images of bedding and pillows and thought we knew why the mirror was up there. But didn't people usually close their eyes? Besides, wouldn't it be too dark to see anything?

From the bed, our attention turned to a circular, tiled, thickly-walled vat in the middle of the bedroom floor. On closer inspection, it turned out to be a pedestaled bathtub and Jacuzzi combination that could have accommodated as many as four or five people. "Do you have any idea what's gone on in there?," she asked. No, and it was a good thing for me that I didn't.

Next, we moved cautiously into the bathroom with its rows of light bulbs; gaudy, gold plumbing fixtures; and mirrors on almost every flat surface. After adjusting to the fun-house effect of mirrored reflections inside mirrored reflections, we opened the medicine cabinet and confronted an array of unfamiliar, oddly-shaped gadgets that had been placed there by the management or, more likely, left behind by previous guests. For several seconds, we were stumped.

Just then, my wife remembered reading an article about how the genital herpes virus can live for as many as eighteen hours independently of the human host. I glanced at my watch; it was not quite 3:00 p.m.; check-out time had been 12:00 noon; and not for another 15 hours could we be sure that this place wasn't crawling with thousands if not millions of unseen microorganisms.

Secretly, I had been amused by the mirror on the ceiling, the bathtub in the living room, and the gizmos in the medicine cabinet. But genital herpes was something else entirely. After all, if I did contract that incurable virus, would my wife later remember that I got it from something like a hotel light switch?

Without wasting another second, she instinctively knew what to do. While I unpacked our bags and started to prepare for the magic show later in the evening, she pulled out the extra rolls of toilet paper from underneath the bathroom sink; she called housekeeping for a load of additional towels; and, with impressive speed, she draped almost everything likely to be touched with a protective layer of cloth or paper. When she finished, the rooms were not, to use a common motel term, "sanitized," but they were well insulated, "for our protection."

Before that moment, I had never believed in Biblical prophesy; however, *Revelations* 22:14-18 warns that "idolaters, fornicators and magicians" will be banished from the proverbial "City of Righteousness" and then, for their wickedness, punished with "plagues." Maybe there was some truth to all that old Sunday school mumbo jumbo after all because there I was — a magician in the world's densest concentration of idolaters and fornicators and I might already have contracted genital herpes from a damned doorknob.

Despite towels, toilet paper and the threat of viral infection, we managed to pull ourselves together and drive to the French restaurant where the shopping center executives were eating and expecting an after-dinner demonstration of mental magic. As billed, I "read" minds, revealed cards people were thinking of, told spectators whom they had gone to grammar school with, and predicted headlines for the *Las Vegas Review Journal*. But there was a problem.

Just before I was to go out on stage, I accidentally dropped a tiny, flesh-colored gimmick, called a "nail writer", on the floor of the dressing room, which was really no more than a dingy, poorly-lighted lavatory. Since I could not do the show without this minuscule but vital prop and since I could not see it anywhere in the gloom, I panicked, dropped down on my hands and knees and started feeling around on tiles that obviously had not been cleaned in quite some time.

Then it struck me: back at Fantasy Tower there were towels and toilet paper for protection but here there was nothing between me and the floor of this unclean Las Vegas men's room. With that thought in mind, I could almost feel the viruses marching on my nether regions.

Back home in Phoenix, I spent the next several weeks neurotically self-absorbed, fretting over the slightest itch, drip, delay or dysfunction. Not knowing exactly what symptoms to look for, I even worried about blurred images on our television set.

In the end, we were fortunate. Neither one of us came down with genital herpes and we both survived our thirty-six hours among the idolaters, fornicators and viruses of Las Vegas. All we needed were towels, toilet paper, and a little magic.

Moving Out

It is Valentine's Day and, a few hours ago, I left my wife. After 25 years of marriage and three children, I packed up some necessities and moved for the first time in two decades. There were no waiting arms or steamy expectations, only sadness over ending a relationship that had lasted so long but also relief about doing something that had once seemed unthinkable. Until I can find a place, I'm staying at a guest house that is owned by one of my law partners and that my wife ruefully calls a "resort." It comes with pine wood floors, a kitchen, Navajo rugs, built-in stereo system, English music hall posters, maid service, early morning coffee and even an extensive wine cellar hidden behind a secretly-hinged bookcase. For the next several days, this is where I'll mooch, sleep, write, feel sorry for myself, and start living alone.

Unlike the classical melodramas about divorce, our marriage did not end with a hurled coffee pot, shouted epithet or sexy interloper. Instead, it died silently during years of a deferential, sometimes craven civility that masked unspoken frustrations, bottled-up hostilities and undisclosed needs. Translation: we couldn't talk about anything personal.

Instead of laying needs, angers or frustrations on the line, we resorted to a system of codes that, by comparison, would have made diplomats sound like blunt talkers. For example, a much-too-cheerful "sure" meant "okay, if you really want to, but I don't like the idea." An unresponsive silence communicated either "no" or "I'm really pissed off," depending upon the context and the body language. Unfortunately, our codes went back a long way.

In the early 1960's we met at Stanford Law School where I had gone as an alternative to the draft and where she had enrolled to learn techniques for constitutional reform. One of the few women in law school in those days, she was intensely private, politically idealistic, and a social loner with a reserve that reflected her austere New England upbringing and with a striking, dark-eyed beauty that was the talk of the male student body.

I was from rural Idaho and the son of a sometimes violent, often alcoholic, and always workaholic physician father who intimidated me from expressing feelings but who pressed me into becoming a driving, over-achieving perfectionist. When it came to externals, I was voluble, outgoing, and relentless. When it came to internals, I was contained and disciplined.

During our courtship, we hardly ever discussed anything personal but, then, we didn't have to. It was, after all, the 60's and almost every day there was something engrossing for two politically-idealistic law students to talk about — bloody confrontations in the South; a raging Vietnam War; resistance to the draft; campus riots; an activist Supreme Court; and an environment poisoned with DDT, phosphate, lead and hydrocarbons. Why discuss intimacies when Vietnamese were being napalmed, Americans were killing and getting killed, civil rights workers were being arrested, and demonstrating students were being clubbed?

Maybe hippies could "let it all hang out;" but we were older; we didn't suck on sugar cubes laced with LSD; we didn't wear long hair or psychedelic rags; and we were still the inhibited, buttoned-down children of the Eisenhower Administration, *Ozzie and Harriet* and *Father Knows Best*. It is hardly surprising that, as children of the 1950's, we associated open expression with weakness, rudeness, and discomfort.

After law school, we got married; I joined a large law firm; she had babies; she didn't work outside the home; and we continued to oppose the War, fight for racial justice and defend free speech. Yet, when the world calmed down, our focus shifted not to ourselves but rather onto our two biological sons and, later, one adopted daughter. Eventually, years went by without an honest discussion of what she really wanted — distance and support for independent fulfillment — and what I really wanted —

closeness and a refuge from my competitive battles.

Yet, without direct discussion, we knew instinctively what the other needed. Without exchanging a word, we could have given each other what was needed and unspoken. But we didn't and, sitting in my partner's guesthouse, I am trying to understand why.

Marital change, it seems, cannot occur without the affirmative acts of voicing, listening, and dealing frontally with each other's truths. As if governed by quantum physics, bottled-up, marital emotions do not just dissipate into nothingness; instead, they become an energy field that, if not released through articulation, ventilation, and resolution, will overheat and melt down the human containment vessels like living, breathing Chernobyls.

In time, my meltdown came, causing nightmares, indigestion, headaches, insomnia and, eventually, an aching, despairing darkness. When the symptoms became acute, I "got help" and was diagnosed as being chronically depressed. So long as the therapeutic focus was on work, toilet training or my father, I was able to sit, lie, talk, and occasionally blubber my way through one psychologist and five psychiatrists. However, whenever a shrink pried into my marriage, I changed the subject or quit. Meanwhile, my darkness got darker.

After I survived what one doctor described as "suicidal ideation" and was told to "talk with your wife," I dragged her to a plump, chatty marriage counselor who could not get us to talk to each other but who liked to hand out her friends' business cards for such ancillary services as massage, mediation, and sex therapy. When that didn't work, we turned to a savvy, caring clergyman and we worked with him for years through separate sessions, joint sessions, diagrams, priority lists, enrichment techniques, action agendas, communication protocols, and behavioral modification strategies. Still, we didn't talk.

In time, I had another, even closer call with "suicidal ideation" and, badly shaken, I saw a new psychiatrist who was not subtle. "Your depression undoubtedly has some genetic and childhood causes," he bluntly explained, "but the deadlock in your marriage is not only exacerbating your condition, it might well push you over the edge." After getting my attention, he went on: "The question isn't morality but functionality and your relationship with your wife is dangerously dysfunctional, even though both of you are decent people and dedicated parents."

"I want you to go onto Prozac immediately," he directed, handing me a prescription. "Even though you'll probably feel better on this medication, please look upon it as a form of emotional Novocain." He continued: "You need to do more than just take pills; you must restructure your life." "More than anything else," he emphasized, "you've got to get unstuck."

Thirteen months later, the marriage counselor advised that "nothing will change" and, at age 50, I decided to do the unthinkable. The decision didn't happen suddenly, like a blinding epiphany. Rather, it came to me over a several-month period as the slow revelation of a deeply-buried truth. Peeling away one layer of resistance after another, I went from the initial abhorrence of leaving to the lesser frets about packing, finding new quarters, wondering where I could buy shower curtains, and worrying about cooking something as simple as a bowl of chili. Once I overcame these mundane impediments, the decision had been made.

Because of our years of marriage counseling, I assumed that my wife and I could at least discuss the mechanics of my proposed departure and that she might even help me pack or find an apartment. I also reasoned that our children would not be troubled because our sons were adults and our twelve-year-old daughter was preoccupied with developmental difficulties of her own. I was wrong.

When the subject of separation first came up, my wife did not react with any detached acceptance and was not mollified by the pledge of economic fairness. Even though I repeatedly assured the children that I loved them and "that I will always be your father," our daughter wailed, "why do you hate mommy?" and our sons reacted to the telephoned news by hanging up in obvious pain.

Unable to improve anything by staying on, I resolved to go as soon as possible. Consequently, my wife left the house for a negotiated period of two hours so that I could pack up my things and move in the manner she thought I deserved — alone.

All by myself except for our pet spaniel, I wandered throughout our four-bedroom house in a daze, staring at over 25 years of accumulated possessions and wondering what to take or even where to begin. After an hour of this crippling melancholy, I started to panic at the prospect that she would return and find me standing in our bedroom, helplessly immobilized and surrounded by scattered heaps of clothes, shoes, medicines, books, sheets, documents and towels. Finally, with a surprising surge of energy, I broke out of my gloomy deadlock and devised a packing system so seemingly effective that I suspected Allied Van Lines or Bekins would have eaten their corporate hearts out to copy it.

Entire drawers of "hard" objects — such as toiletries, documents and cassette tapes — were dumped upside down into large, differently colored legal briefcases. My black briefcase marked "trial exhibits," for example, became a mobile medicine cabinet and brimmed with loose cans of shaving cream, razors, aspirin bottles, hemorrhoidal remedies, toothpaste, and expired pills from forgotten illnesses. Tax returns, bank statements and cancelled checks, which I was anxious to analyze for the financial consequences of my move, were emptied wholesale into the brown briefcase that still carried baggage claim tags from a recent trip to Chicago.

Anything "soft" — such as clothes, shoes and towels — went into plastic laundry bags that I had collected from different hotels during years of business travel. On the theory that all of my old, ill-fitting clothes would be at the bottom of every dresser drawer, I did some strip-mining, removed four handfuls from the top strata of each clothing group and then crammed each wad into the various hotel laundry bags.

When I was finished, the Waldorf-Astoria bag contained underwear; the Ritz-Carlton was stuffed with shirts; the Hyatt-Regency held pants; the

77

Mayfair was for socks; and the Four Seasons bulged with some clammy, unwashed exercise togs. At the last minute, I remembered my shoes and shoved them into the Fairmont bag, which seemed appropriate because I love to walk in San Francisco.

After loading up the car, I concluded my decades-long residency with a maudlin, farewell tour of the house where I had spent nearly half my life. My stops included the hallway wall where there was a framed newspaper article about how we, a Caucasian family of four, had adopted a beautiful Afro-American girl; the living room where Christmas trees had stood and two teenage boys had wrestled; our daughter's room with its dolls, puzzles, and artwork; our sons' rooms with athletic paraphernalia, college textbooks and prom photos; and, finally, the kitchen where I said goodbye to our dog who had given us affection even when my wife and I couldn't give it to each other.

Once inside my partner's guest house with a train of legal briefcases and hotel laundry bags, it became apparent that neither Allied nor Bekins would be interested in my moving system after all. While the coding based upon different hotel bags and briefcase colors had worked, the "strip-mining" and "drawer-dumping" techniques had not. Some underwear was a size 36 and, over the past three years, I have been a size 40; I had packed socks for exercise but none for business; some of my shoes were not in pairs; the tax returns from 1989 and 1990 were missing; and there were no razor blades anywhere.

After a quick inventory of my assorted possessions, I searched the guest house for closets, hangers and shelves and, in the process, noticed my partner's impressive home computer, Moulin Rouge poster, and Native American basket collection. Although I wondered how he could live so well, my concern was not his affluence but my impending poverty. Specifically, how was I going to pay for our sons' college costs, our daughter's medical expenses, my wife's support and my own needs?

Once the clothes, books and shoes were put away, I unpacked the brown briefcase and took out our financial records. To estimate the potential impact of this move in dollars, I studied some economic forecasts from my law firm, divided my reduced income projections by two, and then doubled last year's expenses. It would be easy to cut out vacations in Aspen, donations to alma maters, and fine dining. But what about the mortgage on the house and the rent on an apartment? Despite all my brave talk about maintaining standards of living for everybody, hard times were ahead.

Then, gradually, from somewhere — maybe from the Prozac or from the counseling or from my own inability to absorb any more pain — came a calming certainty that I had done the right thing. Pouring myself a glass of pinot noir from my partner's wine cellar and listening to Vivaldi's "Four Seasons" from the guest house stereo system, I realized that there would be scarcities and hurts; but I also knew that our children were loved, that my wife needed liberation from me and that I could not go on being silent and lonely.

Raising the wine glass, I gave myself a solitary toast. Maybe I wasn't happy but I felt better. I was, it seemed, unstuck.

My Son The Lawyer

Dear Tom:

On Saturday, October 19, 1996, you will be sworn in as a member of the State Bar of Arizona. You may wish to remember that date in the years to come. It will be the anniversary of your entrance into a great profession.

You have been blessed with intelligence, diligence, education, and opportunity. And, you will have, I am sure, an interesting and rewarding career in the law.

Nobody may have told you this and, if they have, it probably did not sink in because it is something most of us have forgotten or have never even stopped to think about: Lawyers have power. Consequently, you, as of Saturday, will have power.

Please understand that your power will be very real. It will be officially vested in you by the state and federal governments and it will be unofficially accorded to you by society in general. Indeed, the reason why lawyers are so often scorned and made the butt of hostile jokes is not that some of us are bad or unethical because there are bad and unethical people in all professions. Rather, it is because we have significantly more power than most other citizens and we sometimes abuse that uncommon power.

Just think after you are sworn in on Saturday, you could draft a complaint; fill it with destructive blather; name anybody or any institution as a defendant; file it next Monday with the court without anybody's consent; trigger toxic publicity; and destroy a reputation, marriage, business, savings, or future that took a lifetime or many lifetimes to build. You, single-handedly, could do all that before the judicial system could finally get around to dealing with what you had filed and before the media eventually would report the outcome in a back-page squib hidden away among ads for trusses and dating services.

Next Monday, you could also have a subpoena issued from the court to anybody within range. You could force the person you subpoenaed to appear at your convenience in your office or at court where you could cross-examine the daylights out of him or her without their permission. It happens all the time.

Although your power could be extreme if you became a criminal prosecutor who indicts or a judge who extinguishes life itself, the power I'm talking about can be far more subtle than that and it is not restricted to lawyers or judges who handle litigation. For example, transactional lawyers can cut corners in their due diligence, withhold vital information, undermine public markets and fleece investors out of their hard-earned savings. Moreover, all lawyers, whether litigators or non-litigators, hold the power that comes from knowing client secrets which, if divulged, could create incalculable problems.

Given all this new power that you are about to have, I commend to you a negative exhortation which new physicians have been hearing for centuries and which new lawyers should hear as well. In Latin, the negative exhortation is, *"Primum non nocere."* Translated into English, it is, "First, do no harm!"

For lawyers this commandment does not mean that we should be timid or wish-washy or shrink from ethically and zealously representing our clients just because there may be pain or loss or controversy ahead. Rather, it means that we should never abuse our power or use it mindlessly or for purely destructive purposes no matter what the personal, financial or professional incentives might be.

If you make this commandment your credo and if, before you take any precipitous legal step, you ask yourself whether you are doing harm, then you will care well for your clients. At the same time, you will elevate your profession and ennoble yourself.

Congratulations, I am very proud of you.

Love, Dad

The Night The Police Came

When the doorbell to my apartment rang about 9:45 at night, I assumed it was my estranged wife who had come to pick up our thirteen-year-old daughter. But I was wrong. At the door were two police officers.

"Are you Peter Baird?" The younger officer sounded grave. "Yes."

"Are you Kendra Baird's father?" "Yes." My heart raced. "Do you mind if we come in and ask you a few questions?" I knew, from having defended criminal cases, that there were hazards in speaking to police officers without foresight or counsel. But they knew my daughter's name and so I mumbled an "Okay." and stood aside. With their wide belts laden with revolvers, cartridges, handcuffs, mace, and nightsticks, they walked through the darkened foyer and into a lighted hallway, making jangly, leather noises with every step. "Has something happened to Kendra?," I asked. In the light, they looked surprised to see that I was an overweight, bald Caucasian in my 50's. Evidently, they already knew that my daughter was a beautiful African-American teenager because they gave me that how-does-he-fit-with-her look I had seen hundreds of times in the past.

They didn't answer my question and, instead, the younger officer said, "A neighbor of yours, someone who wants to remain anonymous, called about twenty minutes ago and said that Kendra was there, crying hysterically."

"What?"

"Kendra's outside, down the stairs with her mom. We've talked to both of them and I'm sure you know that child abuse is serious business." Before the words "child abuse" could sink in, he jarred me with this: "Kendra told us that you beat her tonight and that she had to jump off the balcony of your apartment to get away."

All I could say, again, was, "What?" Then, suddenly, my stomach turned to ice as I envisioned friends, clients, partners, and judges reading headlines about, "PARTNER IN PROMINENT PHOENIX LAW FIRM CHARGED WITH CHILD ABUSE."

The sergeant spoke for the first time. "We couldn't see any marks or bruises on her but clothes often cover areas where kids get beat." He paused. "Why don't you tell us what happened?"

"What happened" had started thirteen years earlier when we adopted Kendra and she was three months old and we were almost forty and our biological sons were nine and eleven. There was no hint of any problem and soon we were talking about Stanford for her intelligence, Olympics for her gymnastics, and fashion-modeling for her dark eyes, cocoa skin, and brilliant smile. Yet, by the time she was five, her precocities had started to fade.

"Mr. Baird, are you going to talk to us?"

"Yes, I'll talk." I took a deep breath and some comfort from the fact that Kendra's mother was just outside. Since I lived anonymously alone in an apartment complex rather than in the upscale, four-bedroom house where the neighbors had known us for over two decades, I assumed that my estranged wife would vouch for me despite the crumbling of our twenty-five-year marriage.

But then, before I could speak, the younger officer said, "We understand from Kendra's mom that this has happened before."

"*This* has happened before?" "This," meaning that I had abused my daughter before? What was my wife talking about? Obviously, it was time for me to say something more than just another, "What?"

Stammering at first, I told the police about my clash with Kendra earlier in the evening when she had stolen a friend's gerbil. As punishment, I had confiscated her "Caboodle," a pink plastic chest filled with cheap cosmetics and costume jewelry.

Deprived of her most treasured possessions, Kendra called me vile names; I banished her to her room; she resisted with more trash talk; and then, after my shoving and her scratching, I locked her into the bedroom where I assumed she was cooling down and listening to a blaring rock station. Evidently, she must have opened the door from her bedroom to the balcony, jumped off and run to a neighbor's apartment, crying and accusing me of child abuse.

"So you didn't beat her tonight?"

"No, sir."

"But your wife said that this had happened before and —"

I cut him off. "By 'this,' she must have meant that Kendra had called the police before." Indeed, the last time Kendra had summoned the police, I explained, was when her mother had refused to buy her brownie mix at the supermarket.

The officers exchanged puzzled glances and tried to make sense out of a story that involved a stolen gerbil, brownie mix, a "Caboodle," a biracial family and allegations of child abuse. Meanwhile, I went on to say that, even though she was loving and beautiful, Kendra had emotional problems and, in the past, had run away, broken windows, kicked in doors, stolen jewelry, threatened her brothers with knives, and accused us of everything from "hating" her to "strangling" her.

Then I remembered the letter and walked to the kitchen, pulled open a drawer and pawed through some loose papers. After several frantic moments, I found a "To Whom It May Concern" letter that had been written by one of Kendra's physicians and that I handed to the sergeant. In it, the doctor described how Kendra lost control and called the police.

Tragically, that letter was one of many reports we had from a battery of pediatricians, psychiatrists, neurologists, and psychologists. Early on, the diagnosis had been "attention deficit hyperactivity disorder" or "ADHD" and the prescription was Ritalin. Later, after she was neurologically evaluated at Boston Children's Hospital, the doctors concluded that, when Kendra's birth mother was pregnant, she must have taken a drug that impaired the proper development of Kendra's brain.

Once the officers read the letter, they became friendly, sympathetic, almost apologetic. They wanted Kendra's medical information in the department's computer so future calls could be answered by informed officers. The sergeant had himself raised a hyperactive child who had put him "through hell."

After the police left, I poured myself a glass of straight scotch and wondered how close I had came to arrest, disgrace, and professional ruin. With a surge of my own hyperactivity, I berated myself for over-reacting to the names Kendra had called me; I cursed my wife's reported ambiguity; I railed at Kendra's birth mother; and I spent the next two hours asking myself hard questions.

Was it just a matter of time before Kendra would again call the police? If so, would she make sexual allegations I couldn't disprove? Would our divorce aggravate Kendra's condition? Should I hire an adult baby sitter for the times Kendra and I would be together? If her problems got worse, where would the money come from since my insurance covered only a fraction of her expenses?

Yet, I am Kendra's father and the one thing my wife and I did agree on was that the words "father" and "mother" were not just nouns, they were also verbs that meant changing diapers, getting up in the middle of the night, cleaning up messes, and being there despite the circumstances, costs, or risks. More than most children, Kendra needed a father, a real one, to help her through hurts, eruptions, special schools, expensive treatments and, occasionally, being called "nigger."

But as a noun or a verb, did "father" require me to risk unfounded criminal charges and jeopardize my reputation, career and livelihood? How could I balance her need for a father with my own need for self-preservation? Could I be an effective father with a baby sitter present? How did my responsibilities to two sons, estranged wife, clients, and law partners figure into the equation?

By the time the questions stopped, it was almost midnight. After I put away the scotch and climbed into bed, it dawned on me that, never once, had I regretted adopting Kendra and never once had I been tempted to abandon her. Black or white, divorced or married, biological or adoptive, one-on-one or with a sitter, I am Kendra's father. Somehow, some way, I'll be her noun and her verb.

Watching Sex Videos With My Wife

For decades, *The New York Times Book Review* has enriched my Sundays with cultural erudition and interesting information. When I am reading those limp pages, I often feel the way I did in college when I first heard words like "solipsism," read books like *Being And Nothingness*, or struggled with conundrums like "Xeno's Paradox."

Consequently, when I opened the *The New York Times Book Review* expecting another intellectual fix, I was stunned to encounter a full-page ad for "SEX EDUCATION VIDEOS THAT INCREASE SEXUAL PLEAS-URE FOR BOTH PARTNERS." Startled that *The Times Book Review* would carry such an ad, I began reading the text which promised "visual excitement, sexual intensity, emotional intimacy;" "heights of ecstasy most people only dream about;" "advanced sexual positions" for fast learners; "*www.bettersex.com*" for the computer literate; and "Express Delivery" for those in heat or a hurry. As if that were not enough, the ad carried a photograph of an attractive, nuzzling couple who were certainly not discussing solipsism.

Intrigued and embarrassed at the same time, I self-consciously turned to the Best Seller Lists and tried to dismiss this unsettling advertisement from my mind. The videos had to be pornographic; *The Times* had to be strapped for revenue; or maybe a new advertising director had just come over from *Playboy Magazine*. Even if any of those assumptions were correct, I was sure that the advertisement would never appear again because *The Times* readers had to be just like me — too refined or too repressed to pay for carnal tutoring.

Yet, to my amazement, the ads continued in subsequent issues and, to my further amazement, they later appeared in *The New Yorker*. When *The*

Atlantic followed suit, I started to think that, since these high-brow magazines were running the same ads, maybe the videos were "educational" after all, perhaps they were even "therapeutic." In any case, they couldn't be smut.

So I read the ad fully and was impressed that the videos had been developed at the "Sinclair Institute" by "educators and counselors" and that they were "used in universities and recommended by family doctors, gynecologists, psychiatrists and sex therapists." Even more important, the men and women in the tapes weren't pros or perverts; they were "real," "typical," "ordinary couples." Indeed, the ads boasted, "ORDINARY COUPLES, EXTRAORDINARY SEX."

That line resonated with me because, in our 60's, my wife and I are an ordinary couple who hardly have the time or opportunity for any kind of sex. One of us is too tired; the telephone rings at the wrong time; somebody's at the door; work isn't done; one of the kids has us worried; an argument isn't over; or the Gods of Virility have forsaken me. Maybe the "educators," "counselors," and "ordinary couples" at the "Sinclair Institute" could help get us back on track.

With my wife's willing consent, I called the 800 number but felt uneasy about it. The ads promised "Plain Packaging Protects Your Privacy" but was that true? Would the Sinclair Institute sell my identity to sleaze merchants? Would my credit card get charged for a stranger's assignation in Las Vegas or day-long call to South America? Would throaty voices call in the night? Would postal inspectors flash badges in my face?

With those questions on my mind, I stammered through placing an order but, before hanging up, I happened to ask if my name and address would be sold or given out to anybody. After some hesitation, the salesperson responded, "it could happen unless the customer specifies otherwise." Immediately, I specified otherwise.

In time, the videos arrived and, wasting little time, my wife and I loaded the VCR, climbed into bed and stared at the screen, rapt. The first people we met were the narrators: a male physician from Duke and a female psychologist from the University of Connecticut. Their credentials were impressive. So far, so good.

After telling us how "the mind is the most powerful sexual organ," the narrators then introduced "Donald and Barbara," "Larry and Hue" and "April and Michael" who, for reasons that would soon be apparent, had no last names. They were so handsome, fit and unabashed that it was hard to believe they were "ordinary couples."

Once the introductions had ended, one couple after another appeared in the raw and performed various demonstrations, sitting, standing, lying down; backwards, forwards and every which way; on beds, floors, and hearths; through pools, showers, and baths; and with shaving cream, feathers, and even strawberries. When they came up for air, their talk was not about love, their expressions were vacant and they could easily have been thinking about dental appointments or grocery lists.

Bug-eyed and embarrassed, my wife and I sat there silently as a zoom lens took us closer to the couples' nether regions than we were to our own. After gaping slack-jawed, we started mumbling, "Oh-my-god-what-are-they-doing?"

After about ten minutes, we started to giggle as each lascivious antic became funnier than the one before. Eventually, when one partner started "grooming" the other's privates with a razor, we erupted into gales of laughter.

Abruptly, my wife stopped and said, "There's no cellulite."

"What?," I asked.

"Those ordinary women don't have cellulite, sags or wrinkles and their skin is tight and their boobs are perfect." Rather than getting aroused, she had looked for something ordinary and didn't find it.

Coincidentally, I had done the same thing. Instead of getting turned on, I had compared my own sorry hide with the studs thrashing away on screen. None of them had love handles, paunches, or anything that wasn't divinely blessed by the Gods Of Virility.

Obviously, these weren't "ordinary couples" at all and we had been gulled by one of the oldest tricks in the book. Just as carnivals once charged rubes to see "educational" nudity inside the tent, the Sinclair Institute had sold us videos that were funnier than the Marx Brothers but hardly educational in any academic or intellectual sense.

In other words, the joke was on us and that was funnier than the videos and we started laughing again. For what seemed like a long time, we rolled around on the bed with our sides splitting until, eventually, we ran out of breath, fell into each other's arms and, in a very ordinary way, made love.

CHAPTER FOUR

WRITER
SHORT FICTION, LONG FICTION
AND LITERARY REJECTION

Guns

Beyond Peleliu

Overnight In Seattle

Rejectionology

Guns

At first, I couldn't understand why my father liked to shoot. After all, it was a bullet, fired by a Japanese sniper on Okinawa, that had shattered his left hand; forced him to live with a metal-splinted claw; made impossible a promised residency at the University of Chicago Hospital; and drove him, in 1947 when he had no surgical prospects, to answer a "Desperate For Doctor" ad in *The Journal of The American Medical Association*. Since no other physicians applied, he got the job and moved us from Evanston, Illinois to the remote lumber town of Headquarters, Idaho, population 843.

There, at the end of a seventy-six mile gravel road that snaked along the Coeur d'Alene River and that climbed into the high Shoshone Mountains of Idaho's northern panhandle, patients didn't care about medical boards; the closest physician was over two hours away; and my father could bury his professional frustrations in hunting, drinking, and doctoring as best he could with four left fingers that were between 80% to 90% immobile. As everyone in town soon learned, his doctoring and drinking were connected.

Life in Headquarters revolved around the saw mill and was scripted, down to the price of milk at the company store and the color of paint on the company houses, by the Montana-Idaho Timber Corporation, or "M-I," which owned everything, including the six-bed hospital, and which employed everybody, including my father. As part of its compensation package, M-I provided my father, mother, and me with a split-level house built into a hillside that overlooked a front driveway and, in the distance, the Coeur d'Alene River.

In the late afternoons after grade school was out, I would sit in front of the large, upstairs picture window and watch for my father's approaching Buick. If things had gone well at the hospital that day, then he'd come home right after the five o'clock mill whistle, eager to shoot clay pigeons with me in our backyard.

But sometimes he didn't come home on time and that usually meant he couldn't save the legs of a logger crushed by a falling, ten thousand pound Ponderosa, the arm of an edgerman sliced open by a high-speed saw, or the life of a mill worker mangled in the green chain. For the gravely injured, my father could do little more than inject morphine, stanch the bleeding, rig up an IV, and, as soon as possible, send the moaning victim off by ambulance to Spokane or Moscow where, as he put it, "there were real surgeons with two hands and ten fingers."

Each time an ambulance sped off with its siren wailing and dust billowing, my father would retreat to his office and start to throw down "depth charges," a wartime combination of straight bourbon followed by beer chasers. Gradually, the rage that he had brought home from Okinawa would displace the pangs of self-loathing and, for a period of hours or sometimes days, he would be out-of-control, violent, and cruel.

Amid great clamor, there were middle-of-the-night homecomings, car wrecks, black eyes that forced my mother into temporary seclusion and bruises that I explained away at school as having come from fights with other kids. Yet, by some process I still don't understand today, my eight-year-old mind could block out his boozy assaults as if they hadn't even happened. Back then, all that registered with me were those other, delicious moments when, sober and attentive, he would come home and unlock the gun cabinet.

For target practice, there was a pump .22 rifle. For deer, there was a lever-action Winchester like those fired in western movies. And, for birds and rabbits, I used a bolt-action .410 and he preferred a heavy, automatic 12-gauge with intricate hunting scenes etched into the outside of the breech.

Once he had opened up the gun cabinet and we had selected the firearms for that day, then the ritual was always the same: get out the ammo; pack up the car; drive to the marshes, fields or high country; and, before starting to hunt, jointly recite this Marine Corps maxim: "Never aim your weapon at anyone or anything unless you intend to kill it." Together, we joyfully honored that rule, bagging white-tailed jackrabbits, getting "our" deer or elk and downing flushed, ringed-neck pheasants from the rolling wheat fields at the base of the Shoshone Mountains.

Most of all, we loved to hunt ducks and geese. On Saturday mornings in September, we would wake up at 4:30 a.m.; he'd cook burned bacon, toast and scrambled eggs; and, with shotguns and ammo, we'd drive to the downstream marshes of the Couer d'Alene River, carrying a thermos of hot cocoa for me and a jug of coffee for him. Nothing could compare, then or now, to sitting next to my father in the pre-dawn cold of an Idaho duck blind, listening for the distant honkings of an approaching formation of Canadian geese, and sipping hot chocolate.

Unfortunately, there was another weapon in our house. It was a Colt .38 revolver that my father kept in his top dresser drawer beneath folded socks and loose underwear. It was always loaded and the safety was never on. One day, with the well-oiled Colt lying flat on his palm, he warned me never to touch it and explained, in grave tones, why it wasn't locked in the gun cabinet. "If anyone ever breaks in here for the morphine in my doctor's bag, instead of narcotics, the son-of-a-bitch'll get a .38 slug in the left ventricle." With his dead-eye aim and combat-tested ferocity, I knew that he could, and would, stop any intruder with a single bullet to the heart.

In July 1950, word came that the Idaho Board of Medical Examiners would be meeting at the end of the month in Boise to review accumulated complaints about my father's alleged malpractice and binge drinking. Back then, Boise was a hard, sixteen-hour drive downstate from Headquarters and nobody went there unless they had to. As my father saw it, he didn't have to because, "M-1's lawyers will take care of everything." Consequently, when the day came for the Boise hearing, my mother and I drove off to Moscow for shopping and, confident and upbeat, he left for the Headquarters Hospital as usual.

Late that afternoon, my mother and I returned from Moscow with the day's purchases. She parked in the front driveway and we climbed out of the car. I leaned back and stretched after the long drive and she dug in her purse for the key to the front door. Just then, my eye caught some movement behind the living room picture window above us.

I looked up and froze. "Mom," I said and she looked up too. On the other side of the glass was my father, holding the Colt .38 in his right hand and pointing it in our direction. His arm was unsteady and I learned later that a call had come from Boise shortly after lunch about the suspension of his medical license and that he had spent the rest of the day drinking. Motionless and unbreathing, my mother and I just stood there, staring up at the bobbing muzzle and not knowing what was going to happen next.

I only heard the first shot, not the second. Looking back now, there couldn't have been as much flying glass as I thought and the explosion couldn't have been as deafening as it seemed. All I know for sure is that, except for some superficial cuts, my mother and I were unhurt and, suddenly, I had only one parent.

Two weeks later, in August 1950, my mother and I moved back to Illinois. She never remarried and she never forgave him, especially for that second shot. Just before she died last year in an Oak Park nursing home, I tried to put things into perspective and talk about World War Two, Okinawa, the sniper's bullet and forgiveness but she would have none of it. Rather than argue, I changed the subject to the rendition of "Let Me Call You Sweetheart" that someone was playing on a piano down the hall.

It has been more than forty-five years since I cradled a shotgun, flushed a pheasant or pulled a trigger. Still, there are times, in barber shops or in doctors' offices, when, I'll pick up an outdoor magazine and casually thumb through the pages. If I happen to come to a photograph or a painting of a man and boy hunting together, then, in less than a second, my dad and I are back in the predawn cold of an Idaho duck blind; we're both listening for the distant honkings of an approaching formation of Canadian Geese; and I'm sipping hot chocolate — thick, sweet and eternal.

Overnight In Seattle

The last I saw of my wallet was in the cramped lavatory on board United Airlines Flight 722 from Los Angeles to Seattle. I stood up, pulled my trousers back to waist level, punched the flush button and started to cinch my belt when the customary bulge in my right rear pocket suddenly went flat. Maybe, if my hands had been quicker and the site more hygienic, I could have rescued my wallet from the swirling green chemicals. Instead, I froze and stared as it disappeared into the maw of an airborne septic tank.

"You could file a claim with lost and found in Seattle," an amused flight attendant suggested.

"But didn't you just tell me that environmental regulations prohibit any access to the tank?"

"Yes," she said, fighting a grin.

"Then wouldn't it be a waste to file anything with lost and found?"

"Forgive me sir," she said, laughing at the unintended double entendre. "But this is a 'waste' problem."

As the giggly news about a wallet down the toilet spread from row to row, I slumped back into my seat and finished off the scotch that, without cash, I could no longer pay for. When I left L.A., I had hoped the flight would perk me up but now, somewhere over southern Oregon, I felt I was soaking in the same septic tank as my wallet.

"You're depressed, Mr. Fitzgerald," Dr. Frank had told me three hours before my 4:50 p.m. departure from LAX to Seattle. "We're almost out of time but let me see if I've got it right," he said, looking down at his notes.

"Successful lawyer but feel like a failure. Can't concentrate. Miss deadlines. Make stupid mistakes. Think about suicide. Law partners worry about your health and their liability and insist you see me or someone like me. Only child. Grew up in Durango, Arizona. Parents died in a car accident when you were a sophomore in high school. Were stoic and didn't cry." He paused, "How'm I doing?"

"Durango, Colorado, not Arizona."

He mumbled the letters "C-O-L-O-R-A-D-O" as he corrected his notes and then resumed his pronounless drone. "Married. Two children. Marriage in bad shape. Wife resists sex, refuses counseling, likes the big income but not the absences and distractions required to earn the money." Another pause, "Am I still on track?"

"I guess," I said in a leaden voice.

"Never cheated on her because you honor vows. Won't consider divorce because you were raised Catholic. You think about sex with other women all the time and feel guilty about it. You watch sex videos and feel guilty about that too." He put down his notepad and said, "is that about the size of it?"

"Uh huh."

"When you get back from Seattle, I'll put you on an antidepressant. It'll lift your spirits but it'll also suppress your libido which, from the sound of things, isn't something you're going to miss much anyway."

"And I'll be back to my old, happy, obsessive-compulsive self?"

"No," he shot back. "Feel better pills won't do it. You'll still be boxed in by a toxic marriage and you'll still have to deal with your parents' ungrieved deaths." Then he leaned toward me for emphasis. "Your top priority is to do some heavy-duty couples work with your wife."

"I already told you: she won't do it."

"Then separate to get her attention or divorce her to get a life."

"But I vowed —"

He interrupted me. "If you want to be legalistic about it, didn't she promise to love you for better or worse? How's that vow been holding up?"

I ducked the question and said, "I haven't been to Mass since my parents' death but divorce was drummed into me as something unthink-"

"Doesn't Catholicism frown on suicide?," he interrupted me again. "And hasn't that been on your mind as the way out?"

"I don't know what the Church frowns on anymore, doctor," I said, standing up to go. "All I know is that I'm stuck."

He shook my hand, gave me one of those professionally reassuring smiles and said, "Let me send you off to Seattle with a theological question that could affect how fast you get unstuck. I'm not a Christian but didn't Jesus say something about making life more abundant?"

When the captain announced our approach into the Seattle-Tacoma Airport, I wondered how abundant my life was going to be without wallet, credit cards, cash or driver's license. My reservations at the Four Seasons Hotel were guaranteed but how was I going to get there? What about a taxi in the morning to get to the deposition and another one in the evening to get to the airport? Assuming I could charge meals at the hotel, that would only get me through breakfast and then I'd starve for the next 12 hours until my peanuts-only flight back to L.A.

Obviously, I should make a collect call but to whom? My office, which was closed because it was Friday night? My partners, whose unlisted telephone numbers were in my wallet? My opposing counsel, whom I had called a liar yesterday? My wife, whose brother's birthday party was at our house tonight?

Then I remembered: Joe and Inez Hayward lived in Port Angeles, just a ferry ride across Puget Sound. They had been my parents' closest friends in Durango and, after the accident, I had lived with them and their daughters during my last two years of high school. After I left for college, they moved to Seattle and, for the past 32 years, we had exchanged newsy Christmas cards.

"Will you accept a collect call from Tom Fitzgerald?," the operator asked.

"Tommy Fitz? Why of course," Inez said. "Tommy, how are you?"

"I'm fine, Inez. How about you and Joe?"

"Decrepit but ambulatory," she laughed and then asked, "Where are you?"

"I'm at Sea-Tac, just in from L.A. Lost my wallet, cash, credit cards, driver's license, the works."

"Oh my goodness, how'd you do that?"

"Embarrassing story," I said and was relieved she didn't want to hear it. I then asked for help without actually asking for it: "I'm up here on business. . . got a deposition tomorrow . . .I'm kind of stranded . . . ."

"We'll take care of you, Tommy," Inez responded as I knew she would. "Rather than for us to go over there which could take a couple of hours depending on the ferries, why don't I have Sis pick you up and drive you to your hotel? She lives about 20 minutes from the airport and I know she's in because I just talked to her."

"Sis?" The news jarred me. "I thought she lived in Florida with the airline pilot?"

"No, Tommy," Inez said in a sad voice. "That ended like all the rest and she's here in Seattle where we can keep an eye on her."

"What for," I chuckled. "To watch her fall for more unsuitable men?"

"Partly . . . but it's more complicated than that." Inez took an audible breath. "She's not herself sometimes but she's got a good job at University Hospital and her kids are grown and live nearby and I know she would love to see you after all these years. I'll call her right now. What airline did you come in on?"

"United," I said, rattled by the news yet pumped by a sudden adrenaline rush.

"She drives a white Toyota. Ought to be there in half an hour."

Sue Hayward was always "Sis" to me, even before I moved in with her family. She was two years older and had two personas. When she knocked around Durango without make-up in loose plaid shirts with her blonde hair unpermed and free flowing, she looked like one of those fresh-faced, teenage models you see in Lands' End catalogues, waving from a sailboat or smiling from a ski lift. When she dated hunks on the football team or 20-year-old students from Ft. Lewis College, her wholesome girliness receded into precocious sophistication and a tightly clothed body that, according to the male population of Durango High School, "wouldn't quit." In fact, guys were always asking me what I saw of her and did with her behind closed doors and, to my regret, the answer was always "nothing."

Of course I saw her pad down the hall wrapped in a towel and, a couple of times, even glimpsed her nether regions when doors opened too soon or closed too late. Yet, the poundings in my heart and in my own nether region weren't stoked as much by unclad sightings as by our talks about subjects that seemed deep at the time and by our teasing about subjects that did not. In retrospect, I'm amazed that I could have contained my adolescent fevers for two years and I've often wondered whether that self-restraint toughened me up for the past 12 months of celibacy. More than anything else, though, I was relieved that Joe and Inez never knew about my around-the-clock lust for their older daughter.

"TOMMY," Sis yelled, smiling, as she rounded the Toyota and engulfed me.

"It's been a while, Sis," I said, responding with a bear hug.

"It's been a hundred years," she whispered into my right ear. From the way she tightened her coils around me and nibbled on my earlobe, I could tell she was an expert in the carnal arts and that wasn't a surprise. From her parents' Christmas cards, I knew that, during my decades of monogamy, Sis had gone through four husbands and an unreported number of non-husbands.

I pushed her away for a good look. Her complexion had turned as gray as her tousled hair and her once-glistening eyes were shadowed but not from make-up. Although she looked older than I had expected, her face was still smooth and her figure still hadn't quit. In fact, a well-dressed man waiting nearby gave her the eye and me the smile.

As she drove us downtown, the Catholic me, husband me, and good me kept barking injunctions inside my head: "DO NOT talk about intimate subjects. DO NOT tell her about your marriage, celibacy, or depression. And for GOD'S SAKE DO NOT invite her up to your hotel room." For about twenty minutes, I did my best to confine our conversation to news about her sister, parents, kids and new nursing job but, the closer we got to the Four Seasons Hotel, the faster the injunctions dissolved in a flood of adrenaline, testosterone, loneliness and yearning.

When the doorman greeted the Toyota and opened the passenger side door, she turned to me and said softly, "Tommy, I want to spend the night with you."

"Geez Sis, I don't know," I said, sounding like a sophomore in high school.

"Tommy, it's been inevitable since you lived with us in Durango and, at this moment, we each need love from someone we trust, care about, and would never hurt."

Once settled in the 15th floor suite, we ordered cocktails, dinner, and wine from room service and then spent the next several hours talking. Nothing was left out, nothing was glossed over. When our sagas and confessions ended, Sis and I slowly melted into each other. There wasn't any ripping off of clothes or carrying on like crazed weasels. Rather, we made gradual, eye-contact love, joining our past with our present and accepting each other just as we were — flawed, hurting, and uncertain about almost everything. Eventually, we fell asleep until about 1:30 a.m. when Sis touched my shoulder and said, "Thomas?"

"Huh?"

"You are Thomas?"

"Who'd you think it was, Bill Clinton?," I groaned. "Now go back to sleep, Sis."

"You doubt me, don't you?"

The question jolted me and I sat up and saw a Gideon Bible open in her lap. "Sis, what in the hell are you talking about?"

"You doubt I am the Christ?"

I was stunned. "Damn right I doubt you are the Christ."

"Then I will prove who I am." With that, she got up, took four steps over to the window, opened it wide and started to climb out.

The first thing I saw was the story in *The Los Angeles Times* that my wife, kids, partners and clients would read: "Local lawyer, Thomas L. Fitzgerald, is being held for questioning in Seattle after an unidentified naked woman jumped to her death from Fitzgerald's fifteenth floor hotel room." The next thing I saw were Sis' legs swinging out into the night air and then, with the bedsprings giving me a lift, I leaped. For an instant, I panicked that I would push her out rather than pull her in but, luckily, my arms landed around her shoulders and I pulled her back on top of me as I crashed to the floor.

After we untangled ourselves and silently put on our hotel-supplied, terry cloth robes, I gave in and said, "Okay, you're right. I am Thomas and I did doubt you but I don't any more. You are Jesus Christ." Anything to keep her away from windows.

"Come," she said, "and sit beside me and we shall study the scriptures together."

For what seemed like a long time, we sat on the sofa and took turns reading the New Testament out loud while I nursed a gash on my chin from the rescue mission. One of the passages we came across was *John 10:10* which she read to me: "The thief cometh not, but for to steal, and to kill, and to destroy. I am come that they may have life, and may have it more abundantly." I told her how, only hours earlier, Dr. Frank had referred to that same passage and how good a more abundant life sounded.

She thought for a moment and said, "Then you shall have it, Thomas." For the first time, her eyes glistened and her cheeks showed color.

As the night wore on, I steered the conversation onto the subject of baptism and suggested that she go into the bathroom and fill the tub. When I heard the water run, I dialed her parents. It was 3:45 a.m.

"Hullo," came a groggy male voice.

"Joe, it's Tommy Fitzgerald." There was no way to soften what I dreaded confessing and so, with my stomach knotted, I just blurted it out: "Sis and I slept together tonight and she woke up claiming to be Jesus Christ."

Suddenly alert, Joe said, "Just a moment, Tommy."

I heard some muffled conversation in the background and then Inez' voice came on the line. "Tommy, I was going to tell you about Sis when we spoke earlier on the phone but she seemed to be doing so well that I just didn't think you needed to know."

"What the hell's going on?"

"The psychiatrists say it's a disorder that's treatable with medicine, rest, safety and nurturing. Thank God it isn't schizophrenia."

"How did she get like this?"

"Her last husband was a violent drunk who beat her to a pulp almost every night until she finally ran away and came to Seattle."

"I had no idea."

"Of course you didn't and I should have told you and I am sorry." Then in her most motherly voice, Inez said, "I must tell you something: your parents and Joe and I always wanted you and Sis to get married. Even if your time together was just for one difficult night, it's okay, Tommy, it really is okay."

"Thank you, Inez," I said and went limp with her forgiveness.

Then she asked, "Do you see her purse anywhere?"

"Yes."

"Go get it and you'll find a small, round silver case in there. Take out a green pill and a red one. Give them to her. She'll fall to sleep right way and, when she wakes up, she'll be herself again. We'll catch the early ferry and should be there by 7:30 to pick her up."

Beneath the canopied entrance to the Four Seasons Hotel where one half of me was warm from the outdoor heaters and the other half was cold from the Seattle chill, we said our good-byes. Joe gave me some cash and shook my hand. Inez gave me a long hug. And Sis, putting her palms on both sides of my face, spoke straight into my eyes, "Thank you for saving my life last night, Tommy."

"Believe it or not, Sis, you saved mine too."

As the Lincoln glided away, I knew what it felt like to be loved and forgiven and it felt good. Maybe Dr. Frank had a point. Maybe *John 10:10* was right about Jesus Christ. Maybe she had come to make life more abundant.

"A must-read book, not only for those who fought in World War II, but for all of us living in a time of many wars around the globe. This book can be a source of forgiveness and healing for those who inherited the demons of war."

Sister Helen Prejean, Author, *Dead Man Walking* and *Death of Innocents*

Beyond
Peleliu

Peter Baird

PROLOGUE

September 6, 1996

James Douglas McQuade
Hulings Boat Yard
Box 47
Point Arena, CA 95468-0047

Julie Elizabeth McQuade
c/o Mrs. Beth McQuade
1470 Page Mill Road
Palo Alto, CA 94304-1124

Dear Jim and Julie,

Thank you for your letters and concerns but please don't worry about me. It turns out that prison isn't all that bad for a lawyer when his clients are inmates, guards and the Warden himself. Here, I'm the "Bighouse Counsel" and my perks include "Trusty" status, an office, a computer, a law library and a comfortable cell.

Best of all, I've had time to do some research into our family history and, specifically, into the World War II Battle of Peleliu that your grandfather fought. As the enclosed manuscript suggests, I've also done a great deal of writing.

You are not the only ones who have asked why I would risk losing my liberty and my license by taking a life that was, for all practical purposes, over. Even harder for everyone to understand is how I could possibly find peace in a place like this.

As with so many of life's questions, there are no answers, only stories. Partly remembered, partly reconstructed, this is mine.

Love,
Your father

David McQuade
Number 754639-T
Utah State Prison
Draper, Utah 84020

CHAPTER ONE

HOMESTEAD, PENNSYLVANIA
JULY, 1917

In a cramped tenement built decades earlier by the Carnegie Steel Company for its workers and their families, LaRoux McQuade sat at a small kitchen table next to her ten-year-old son who was holding a live frog. The mill's five o'clock whistle had sounded and an industrial night of heavy soot, thick smoke and early darkness had fallen. Beneath an unshaded light bulb, mother and son considered the wax-bottomed tray, scissors, miniature forceps, needles, straight pins, and glass of milk that lay before them.

"Are you ready, Tommy?" LaRoux asked in a quiet brogue. She was tall, thin-faced, gentle in both features and bearing and wore, as she always did no matter the occasion or season, a plain ankle-length skirt, white blouse with puffy sleeves and hair done up in a soft Gibson Girl cushion.

"Oh, yes," he said, as the frog squirmed in his hands.

She reached over and stroked the top of the frog's head. "Okay then, but we must first pith Mr. Frog."

"What does 'pith' mean, Momma?"

She smiled because none of her high school biology students knew what "pith" meant either. "Well Tommy, it's a procedure that will kill Mr. Frog as quickly and humanely as possible so he doesn't feel any pain during our dissection." She went on, "If we didn't do that, we would be cutting open a live animal and that would be called a 'vivisection' and would be cruel."

"But momma, you said that you were going to show me a live heart and, if we kill Mr. Frog, won't his heart die also?"

"I did say that," she said, still smiling because that too baffled her students. "It's a wee complicated but frogs' hearts keep on beating for a time even after they're dead and even after their hearts have been cut — ." Suddenly, she winced and lurched forward and, after some deep breathing, she reached for the milk, took a sip and then another.

For months, LaRoux had coped with stomach ulcers by wearing her "Scottish smile" that concealed clenched teeth. Lately though, her stoicism was no match for the wrenching cramps and debilitating aches that the doctors said warranted surgery before the ulcers started to bleed dangerously. As soon as the McQuades could afford it, she would have the surgery, but it would be in Pittsburgh by a specialist rather than in Homestead by the company doctor whose ineptitude was as well known as his alcoholism.

As Tommy always did when he saw his mother suffer, he recoiled in fear, as much for himself as for her. After her pain seemed to have subsided, he melded his concern about his mother with his curiosity about the frog into a single question and cautiously asked, "If you and Poppa die, will your hearts keep on beating?"

Avoiding the mortality issue, she took another sip of milk. "Oh my no. Poppa and you and I are mammals and our hearts need a constant flow of warm oxygenated blood to keep on beating. Frogs are amphibians and their hearts are different."

"So, how are we going to pith Mr. Frog?" Tommy asked.

"We'll use that needle," she said, pointing. "But first, we must pray that Mr. Frog won't feel any pain and that he'll go to Frog Heaven and that we'll be forgiven for taking his life."

They bowed their heads and LaRoux prayed in a thicker brogue that Tommy heard on Sundays in their Presbyterian Church, "Heavenly Father, please protect Mr. Frog from pain, accept his soul into Your Kingdom and forgive us for taking his life which we do only in the name of science. Amen."

"Amen," Tommy murmured.

LaRoux took the frog in her left hand and, with her right, stuck the needle into its spine and swiftly ran it up and down what she called "his vertebral canal." The frog went limp.

"Mr. Frog is now with God, Tommy," LaRoux said quietly as her son stared at the lifeless amphibian. After more milk, she turned the deceased frog over on its back, pinned its legs to the wax-bottomed tray and, with the scissors, cut the frog's underside open from crotch to head, exposing its entrails.

Tommy was bug-eyed.

"Do you see the pale, bean-shaped structure in the lower belly?"

Tommy nodded.

"Those are his testes and that means he was a boy frog and we were correct in addressing him as 'Mr. Frog.'" As Tommy stared at the frog, she asked, "You know what testes are, don't you?"

He thought he did but shook his head anyway.

Having anticipated his reticence, she explained, in her best biology teacher's voice, that "Mr. Frog's testes make sperm that he puts into Mrs. Frog when they mate and the sperm fertilizes her eggs so that they can then hatch into baby tadpoles." She paused and said, "In boys, 'testes' are called 'testicles'. I believe you call them 'balls.'"

Tommy turned crimson. He wasn't about to talk about "balls" with his mother.

Amused by his embarrassment, she went on. "See the round, worm-like tube that curves around the testes?"

"Uh huh."

"Those are his intestines that you would call 'guts?'"

"I guess."

"Why don't you find where Mr. Frog's heart is?"

He pointed to an area in the upper left chest that was throbbing. Yet he wasn't sure because it was nested among some red lobes and didn't look like a heart to him.

"Those red lobes are Mr. Frog's lungs and liver and a little lower is his gall bladder." Sensing his uncertainty, she said, "You can't actually see the heart itself until we've done a wee more surgery."

With that, she picked up the scissors and proceeded to slowly cut away what she told him was "the pericardial sac." Then, using the forceps, she lifted the severed, beating heart out of the frog's chest and into full view.

Tommy gasped.

"Open your right hand, Tommy." As he did, she gently placed the pulsating organ in his open palm. Then she sat back and, fighting another round of pain, beamed at her son and his happy fascination.

He was transfixed by what his eyes were seeing and what his palm was feeling. Indeed, his own heart was beating faster than the frog's.

LaRoux whispered, "I think I hear poppa in the bedroom. He must have just come back from the mill. Do you want to show him what you have?" She had heard tier husband's heavy breathing that rattled and rasped on inhalation and wheezed and gurgled on exhalation.

Without taking his eyes off the heart, Tommy nodded.

LaRoux quietly stepped out of the kitchen and, moments later, returned with Thomas Douglas McQuade, Sr., who had just gotten off work as Furnace Foreman at The Homestead Steel Works. He was broad-shouldered, but stooped; wide-framed but thin; and his work shirt, overalls, and boots were caked with coal dust and sparkly metal particles. His face was black with soot and he looked like a minstrel peering out through the two white circles where his goggles had been.

"Tommy, me laddie, whatya got there?" his father said in a dense highland brogue.

"Poppa, it's a frog's heart and, look, it's still beating, all by itself!"

Tom and LaRoux exchanged grins and Tom asked, "Where'd it come from?"

"I caught the frog at the Monongahela River this morning and momma pithed him and then she cut his heart right out of him."

Tom coughed up some phlegm and then joked, "Nice that mom finally taught you how to pith." They all laughed at his play on words.

"You like this cutting out hearts kind of thing?"

"Oh, yes, poppa."

"You want to grow up to be a biology teacher like your momma?"

Tommy thought long and hard about his father's question and then turned his face down toward the floor and was silent.

"Tommy," LaRoux asked, "what's wrong?"

Still staring at the floor, Tommy shook his head and started to sob.

LaRoux knelt beside him and said, "Tell us Tommy."

Crying, he said, "I don't wanna be a teacher, I wanna ... wanna. ... be a doctor."

"And why would that be Tommy?," his father asked.

Choking back tears, he said, "So I could make you and momma well."

Eleven days later, LaRoux's ulcers started to bleed badly and she was rushed to the company infirmary for emergency surgery where she died on the operating table. In his autopsy report, the coroner said the surgery was technically successful but, as the company doctor was closing her up, there had been an "inadvertent overdose of chloroform anesthetic that took the patient's life." Presumably intending to exonerate the company doctor, the coroner said, "It is very difficult to maintain the proper level of chloroform during a long surgery" and then added, "everything that could have been done was done."

Seven months later, Tom McQuade's silicosis, contracted from years of inhaling coal dust and steel particles, became so acute that he couldn't work and a week later the Homestead Steel Works terminated him as well as his at-will lease on the company-owned tenement. After losing wife, job, income, and home and having to fight for every gulp of air, Tom McQuade fell into a paralyzing melancholia that put him in the Pennsylvania Asylum For The Incurably Insane where he was lobotomized and numbly vegetated until he died in The Great Influenza Pandemic of 1918.

Tommy McQuade grew up as a ward of the county and was left with nothing more than a fierce determination to be a doctor, a surgeon, a heart surgeon, no matter what. During the next two decades, there would be many "no matter whats" to overcome, including orphanages, foster homes, The Depression, Pittsburgh University at night, digging trenches and pushing wheelbarrows for the WPA, applying for scholarships and waiting, waiting, waiting, always waiting to be a doctor.

Eventually, nineteen years after Mr. Frog's dissection, the Carnegie Foundation awarded him a scholarship to The Syracuse University College of Medicine, in Syracuse, New York. He suspected that the scholarship was the result of belated corporate guilt about his father and workers like him but, nevertheless, Tom was finally on his way to becoming a doctor, a surgeon, a heart surgeon, no matter what.

CHAPTER TWO

CROUSE IRVING HOSPITAL
SYRACUSE, NEW YORK
APRIL, 1940

From the outside, Crouse Irving Hospital didn't look like a hospital. When it was built in 1913, the doctor founders were so worried about its financial success that they had it designed to look like a hotel, just in case. However, inside the patterned brick, Greek portico and Roman pilaster exterior, Crouse Irving was all hospital, complete with antiseptic aroma, wall-to-wall whiteness, public address pages, and the bustle of staffers in white and visitors in mufti.

Inside was also where fourth-year medical student Thomas Douglas McQuade, Jr., had spent his last two years of medical school, rotating through one clinical clerkship after another. The decades spent waiting had left him bald and near-sighted and the years spent digging ditches and pushing loads of wet cement had left him looking like a heavy-weight boxer, easily able to take the hospital stairs, three steps at a time, on his way to the Department of Surgery. He hadn't been this excited since the operation on Mr. Frog.

Tonight, in his last weeks of a surgical clerkship, Tom would finally operate on a living human being. All he had done so far was stand in the operating room, watch, hold retractors, watch, cut sutures, watch, and get dumped on by the lords of surgery with their masks, gowns, gloves, and distempers. Indeed, their badgerings and bad-mouthings had confirmed the old joke that the only difference between a medical student and fecal material is that nobody goes out of their way to step on fecal material. But tonight it would be his turn to cut, clamp, stitch, and tie and, making the occasion even better, his supervisor would be Dr. Wayne Landry, the finest surgeon in the hospital and one of the few nice guys on a faculty steeped in arrogance and impatience.

Earlier in the day, Dr. Landry had called Tom to the emergency room where a 47-year-old male had come in complaining of pain in the belly. After the examination, Dr. Landry diagnosed appendicitis and, with an avuncular smile, told Tom, "Get ready. He's your patient tonight. I've got to supervise another student appendectomy at 6:00 p.m. so let's do yours at 7:30."

Tom returned the smile and, with his heart racing, said, "Don't worry, Dr. Landry, I'll be ready."

"I know you will," the senior surgeon said, patting Tom's back.

For the next four hours, Tom read, re-read and re-re-read the section in *The Atlas of Operative Technique* on appendectomies that he had memorized long ago. Whenever his nervous fidgeting got the best of him and he couldn't concentrate on the dog-eared pages any longer, he would pick up a spool of catgut and, while pacing the halls and ignoring quizzical stares, tie surgical knots on anything with the rough circumference of a human intestine.

When Tom burst into the Department of Surgery at 7:00 p.m. from the stairwell, Dr. Landry was not there. According to a scrub nurse, Dr. Landry had encountered problems while supervising the other student appendectomy. However, Dr. Landry's instructions were that Tom's patient should be anesthetized and everyone should be scrubbed and ready to go and he would be there as soon as possible. For the next ten, fifteen, and then twenty-five minutes, Tom, the nurses and the anesthesiologist made small talk in the operating room shadows while the patient's exposed midsection glowed an alabaster white.

Finally, at 8:15, the supervising surgeon arrived but it wasn't Dr. Landry; instead, it was Brewster F. Napfield, III. Because of his last name, diminutive stature and toxic personality, students called him "Dr. Napoleon" or "Dr. Nap" for short. Making his entrance in a voice much too loud for an operating room, Dr. Napfield announced that "Dr. Landry's operation should have finished a long time ago but the student pulled the stump stitch too tight, broke the stump open and contaminated the peritoneal cavity." Dr. Napfield chuckled, "It's always sepsis season around here when the kids get knives."

Tom scowled beneath his mask. He wasn't a "kid" and, in fact, he was older than Napfield. Not only that, he had seen Napfield operate before and considered him a mediocre surgeon.

"Ready?" Napfield asked in a military tone. After a muttered chorus of "uh huhs," Napfield said, "Let's see if the soon-to-be class valedictorian is as good with his hands as he is with the books." Napfield's expectation was obvious: Tom may be at the top of his class in academics but, like almost all medical students, he would jelly with nerves and bungle the operation.

"Give him a scalpel," Napfield snapped. Tom took the shiny instrument in one hand and, with rubber-gloved fingers on his other hand, drew an imaginary line across the patient's abdomen. Before cutting, Tom shot Napfield a daggered glance of class-based contempt. Napfield was Boston, society, Princeton, leisure, and wealth. Tom was McKeesport, foster homes, Pitt night school, trenches, and wheelbarrows.

Unfazed by the dirty look, Napfield addressed Tom for the first time with an order, "As you open him up, tell me the names of each layer of tissue you are cutting inn the abdominal wall."

"O.K.," Tom mumbled and then swiftly and evenly ran the blade along his imaginary line without the usual beginner's jerks, jogs, stabs or hesitations. While cutting, Tom rattled off "skin . . . fat . . . fascia . . . muscle" and, finally, "peritoneum," the smooth, glistening inner lining of the abdomen.

Surprised by Tom's deft technique, Napfield held the upper hand with a technical question. "Skin, doctor? Around here we use words like, 'epidermis and dermis.' " Before Tom could respond, Napfield said, "Start clamping."

As fast as the nurse could hand him hemostats, Tom applied them to the severed vessels and, again, Napfield was impressed but still expected a blunder.

"Not bad, now let's see you tie." No matter how long and how diligent students practice tying, they almost always do something wrong in their first, real-life attempt. Fingers get greasy with fat; ligatures don't get knotted; ties slip off; and sometimes glove tips get sutured into the patient's wound. Yet, with the speed and dexterity of a blackjack dealer, Tom tied off each vessel.

Napfield was taken aback but rather than issuing a compliment, asked another technical question. "You know what portion of the bowel the appendix is attached to, Dr. McQuade?"

"Yeah," Tom said, "it's the cecum."

"That's right. So go get it and pull up the appendix." Napfield recalled his own first time trying to locate the damned cecum: he couldn't see it; he had reached into the slick intestinal folds where everything felt like everything else; the first thing he pulled up was a section of the small intestine; the next thing he came out with was the sigmoid colon; and, finally, he gave up and sheepishly asked the supervising resident for help.

Tom nodded and stuck two rubber-gloved fingers through a crease between layered sections of the intestinal hose. In fewer than five seconds, he pulled up the cecum with a hot appendix flopping from it. Agape beneath his mask, Napfield dropped his Dr. Nap persona and watched in deflated silence for the rest of the operation as Tom proceeded to tie off the appendix at its base, cut it off above the tie, invert the stump, hold it in with a purse-string stitch, and then close up the wound with smooth dispatch.

Afterwards in the locker room, Napfield smacked off his gloves, pulled down his mask, and said, "You've got good hands, Dr. Tom McQuade. You'll be a great surgeon someday."

"Thanks."

"By the way, as class valedictorian, what have you decided to do about The Colonic?"

"I haven't decided anything."

Napfield laughed. "Well, you'd better get moving because graduation is just around the corner and we're all waiting to see how you're going to humiliate the shrinks."

CHAPTER THREE

MADAME FORTUNO

At 8:30 the following morning, Tom McQuade dragged himself through the door to his postage-stamp sized apartment. He was too tired from surgery to stay awake but too jangled by coffee to sleep. The place smelled of mildew and kitchen grease and every surface was covered with unwashed dishes, empty cans, medical books, butt-filled ashtrays or dirty clothes. His first thought, as it always had been when he confronted the chaos of his own bachelorhood, was to do something about the stink and the mess but he was well-practiced at deferring action until there was more time, more sleep or more of anything else that happened to come to mind.

His next thought was prompted by the question from Napfield last night and it was one he could no longer put off: What was he going to do about The Colonic? As valedictorian of the medical school class of 1940, tradition required that Tom arrange for the intermission entertainment, called "The Colonic," at the upcoming graduation dinner dance. So far, he had done nothing.

The Colonic was the graduating seniors' opportunity to even the score with a faculty who believed that overloading and browbeating turned sweaty-palmed memorizers into caring physicians and who had, over the past four years, managed to drive one student to suicide, five others into nervous breakdowns and another twenty-seven to drop out altogether. In 1938, for example, the valedictorian had hired a fire-eater to spit flames at members of the ear, nose and throat department. In 1939, circus clowns freakishly costumed as doctors, dragged each surgery professor up on the stage and, using oversized butcher knives and speaking in a venomous operating room argot, "removed" saws, screwdrivers, and even a toilet

121

plunger from the draped surgeons.

The show was called "The Colonic" because chiropractors prescribed "colonic irrigations" and, at Syracuse Medical School, chiropractors were considered charlatans and quacks. Since the medical faculty also believed that colonic irrigations were worthless and sometimes dangerous, their cruelest rebuke was to announce, in class or clinic, that "a colonic would be better" than what the floundering student had just suggested.

This year, it was the Department of Psychiatry's rotational turn for "a colonic" and Tom wanted to do as much satirical damage to them as possible. Because of the lobotomy that had turned his father into a vegetable and himself into an orphan, he bitterly denounced the psychiatrists when he discovered that, in the Syracuse Medical School Department of Psychiatry, lobotomies had not yet gone the way of leeches. Vowing never to let himself or any patient become a vegetable, he expounded publicly to anyone who would listen and many who wouldn't how superior real vegetables were to the human variety because "carrots and turnips don't drool, don't stare at the floor and don't pee in their pants."

Trying to get his mind off The Colonic, Tom switched on the lone floor lamp, flopped down on the disheveled hide-a-bed and picked up *The Syracuse Herald American* in search of spring training baseball scores. He glanced at the front page about the war in Europe and then, thumbing his way to the sports section, caught a headline out of the corner of his eye in the society section that read, "Madame Fortuno Reads Minds of Spring Ball Goers." It seemed there was a mind reader in town and, from her photograph, she was an attractive gypsy who gave "extra-sensory perception" shows. Apparently, she told well-dressed members of Syracuse society what their futures would be, what they were thinking and what the names were of their childhood pets.

Tom sat up, grabbed a coffee-stained telephone directory, riffled through the Yellow Pages, and called each talent agent listed alphabetically until he spoke to a gravely-voiced old timer named Simon Wizanski. According to the agent, he represented Madame Fortuno and, besides that, knew her well because she was a good friend of his daughter. Madame Fortuno gave a great ESP show the agent said; however, he was concerned that she might "overdo the satirical damage" and, therefore, Tom might be happier with "Priscilla the Pretzel," a sexy contortionist who could teach the physicians a thing or two about anatomy.

Since this year's Colonic targeted minds not bodies, he insisted on Madame Fortuno and was pleased that she might "overdo the satirical damage." With Tom's mind made up, Wizanski explained that Tom would have to call Madame Fortuno directly because she screened all jobs that involved, as The Colonic surely would, special arrangements.

Lighting up a Lucky Strike, Tom called the number Wizanski had given him. "Good morning, Syracuse Girls' Club," a cheerful female voice said.

"Is this Central 4577?"

"Yes it is."

"Well, this may sound nuts, but I'm trying to reach someone . . . I think she's a gypsy or something . . . named Madame Fortuno."

"Oh," the receptionist laughed, "you want our director, Virginia Russell. She's Madame Fortuno. I'll connect you."

After several rings, Tom McQuade heard a female voice say, "This is Virginia Russell speaking."

"Uh . . . I'm . . . calling for . . . uh . . . a . . . Madame Fortuno."

"This is she," Virginia said in low-octave tone that Tom thought sounded sultry.

Despite having just heard the words "Syracuse Girl's Club" followed by the unaccented voice of an educated woman, Tom nevertheless imagined the person he was talking to as a bejeweled, dark-skinned foreigner who was, at that moment, hunched over a crystal ball in a heavily draped parlor filled with lighted candles, Tarot cards, and luminous-eyed cats. He was accurate in only one respect: Virginia had light brown skin.

With the telephone to her ear, Virginia sat at her desk in a spacious,

123

well-lighted office with a sweeping view of the Syracuse University campus. Books, photographs and diplomas lined the walls and uneven stacks of paper rose up from her desk. In her early thirties like Tom, Virginia wore a smart, hound's-tooth business suit that couldn't conceal a shapely figure. Her horn-rimmed reading glasses meant business and her black pearl eyes radiated intensity.

On weekends, however, Virginia Russell did resemble the image in Tom's mind. Come Friday and Saturday nights, she rouged up, donned a Gypsy costume, put her hair up in a white bandanna, slipped on heavy gold jewelry and packed two large, leather satchels with a 'nail writer,' an 'add-a-number' pad, a 'force book,' a double-flapped slate, a windowed envelope, a 'billet knife,' heavy crayons, one ping pong ball, a 12" by 18" pad, flash paper, igniters, wires, smoke pots, three small manila envelopes and a specially stacked deck of cards. Once "loaded," Madame Fortuno raised money for the Girls' Club by performing mental magic and spiritual sorcery championed by Sir Arthur Conan Doyle, debunked by Harry Houdini, studied by Dr. J. B. Rhine at Duke University and broadcast to millions each week on CBS Radio by the basso-voiced magician, Joseph Dunninger.

"This is Doctor McQuade calling," Tom said, fudging because he had not yet received his degree.

Virginia Russell looked up at the Seth Thomas wall clock and said, in a business-like but intriguing voice, "Doctor, I'm sorry but I'm in a hurry. Saturdays are very busy around here and I'm due at a budget committee meeting in five minutes. I assume you're calling about Elaine D'Angelo, the little Italian girl who broke her arm on our playground yesterday?"

"Well, no," he admitted. "Actually, I wanted to book your Madame Fortuno act and I just talked to Mr. Wizanski who told me to call you and I wondered if you'd be willing to use your 'mental powers' to lampoon the psychiatry department at the medical school graduation dinner dance on June 8. I read about you in the *Herald American* and I'd like you to 'read' the shrinks' minds and tell everybody what utter fools they are."

Virginia ended the conversation in a hurry. "I'll do the show if the medical school will pay the fee Simon negotiates with you and also donate $20 to the Girls' Club but it'll be my script, not yours. I don't use magic to lampoon or demean anybody, not even doctors. Never have. Never will. If those conditions are acceptable, confirm it with Simon. Thank you but I really must go."

Tom McQuade heard a click and then a dial tone. In seconds, he was back on the line with Wizanski, pumping the agent for information about Virginia Russell, aka "Madame Fortuno." Happy to get the booking but hesitant to talk about Madame Fortuno's background, the agent clammed up and tried to get off the line with three "I gotta goes" and two "I'm lates," but Tom wouldn't let him.

In an emphatic voice that implied consequences, Tom laid it on the line. "'Hey, bub, there's not going to be a booking for Fortuno or a commission for you unless I get some information."

Wizanski thought for a moment and, yielding, said, "O.K. but there are a couple of things you'd be better off not knowing."

"Like what?"

"Like she's part colored for one thing," the agent blurted. Then he quickly added, "but she can pass and nobody can really tell but if this bothers you then —"

"It doesn't," Tom said. He had only one prejudice and that was an automatic hostility against comfortably born, silver-spooners like Napfield. Growing up poor and alone, Tom had a better understanding than most Caucasians about what life was like for Negroes and, until the juvenile officials decided they were "colored," Tom's favorite foster parents "passed" during the day but lived as Negroes nights and on weekends. Tom then asked, "You said, 'for one thing,' is there 'another thing?"'

"Well, there is and it's the reason I was worried that she might 'overdo the damage' at your show."

"That would be great if she did but she said she wouldn't so what is it

I'd be better off not knowing?"

"Well . . . she's a Christian Scientist and isn't very keen on doctors."

Tom thought that was pretty funny. "Tell you what: if she keels over on stage, we'll ignore her, call the undertaker, and go on drinking."

The agent laughed too and was relieved that he had gotten the touchy subjects of race and religion off his chest. With nothing else left that could jeopardize his commission, Wizanski rattled on at length about Virginia Russell. She was raised in a small town in north central Illinois; her father was a prominent lawyer; and her only sibling was a much older sister in Boston. In the early 1800's, the Russell family ancestors had been Abolitionists and had taken in a runaway slave named Molly Sykes whose mystical powers to reveal the past, predict the future and heal the sick were still legendary in that part of Illinois. Lost to history or hidden by discretion was the identity of the father of Molly's son whom she delivered at the Russell house and who became a member of the family, too.

The agent suspected, but didn't know, whether the Molly Sykes stories influenced succeeding generations of Russells to embrace the teachings of Mary Baker Eddy or whether the stories enhanced Virginia's interest in magic. All he knew for sure was that, in 1918 when she was ten, Virginia saw Harry Houdini perform at the Majestic Theatre in Chicago and saw him escape from "The Devil's Death Chamber." After that, she was hooked and, refusing to be a "lovely assistant," she became a ham-handed magician herself, doing the now-you-see-it-now-you-don't type of tricks for anyone who was interested and many more who weren't.

Wizanski knew when, but not how, Virginia had become an accomplished mental magician. What he knew was that, after getting her master's degree in social work from Northwestern University, her first job was in the "colored" cell block at Illinois' Dwight Prison For Women and that's where, somehow, she had learned the arcana of mental magic and the mis-directions of illusion.

What the agent didn't know was that, at the prison, Virginia met

Wanda "The Wizardess" Freeman, a dark, nimble-fingered bunko artist and generously curved prostitute from Jamaica. She was the daughter of a British gambler father and a mulatto cabaret singer mother. Early on, Wanda realized that her father's secrets, her mother's skills and her own body were the tickets to money, adventure and escape. Employing these talents in the casinos and first class cabins of the steamships that plied the waters of the Atlantic and Caribbean, Wanda eventually became the well-cared-for mistress of a wealthy Chicago industrialist. When he died years later and left Wanda nothing, she joined a succession of Midwest carnivals and performed whatever tricks were necessary, both carnal and magical.

In prison for fraud, Wanda was intrigued by Virginia's color and, after learning about Molly Sykes, set out to teach this straight-laced young social worker "real magic." Over the course of a year, Wanda schooled her bug-eyed pupil in "center tears" and "billet switches" ("dumb bastard'll never guess you got his birthday or sweetie's name straight from him"); "nail writers" ("when the mark tells you how much he weighs, just write it down secretly with your thumb, like so, then open the window envelope and he'll think you guessed his weight by looking at his fat ass");" cold reading" ("tell 'em stuff that would fit almost anybody, like they're too hard on themselves or they worry a lot about money"); "forces" ("you can get anybody to take any card or to think of certain things if you do it right"); "smoke pots" ("You can vanish an elephant with them"); and "flash fires" ("they'll illuminate anything"). As a determined teacher, Wanda didn't just show and tell, she drilled and critiqued her student until, the night before Virginia left for Syracuse, she appeared as "Madame Fortuno" and gave a full length show for the entire prison population, confirming earlier predictions, revealing unspoken secrets, setting off dense curtains of smoke and igniting brilliant cones of fire. She was a hit.

The next morning, Virginia and Wanda hugged and wept their respective goodbyes to each other. Dabbing her eyes with one hand, Wanda handed Virginia a farewell gift with the other. "Here's a book I've used for a long time, Ginny. It's got instructions, diagrams, moves, wirings, patter, descriptions, and everything you'll ever need to do your magic and make money for you or for anything or anybody.") Before Virginia could thank her, Wanda shook her head and said, "There's one thing I am sorry about and that is I never answered your questions about men; but, if I had and if the warden had heard that a hooker had corrupted an innocent do-gooder like you, he would have thrown my black ass in the hole for a month."

"That's alright, Wanda," Virginia said with a chuckle. "I really am ignorant of… well… ."

It's O.K. to say 'sex' Ginny girl."

Virginia blushed and mumbled, "sex."

"One more time."

"Sex," Virginia said it loud and clear.

"Much better."

"The problem is that nobody ever talked to me about 'sex' and, if I get married, I'm not sure what I'll do."

"You'll do fine, honey," Wanda said. "Just remember two rules about men." Slipping into a Jamaican patois, she said, "Don't give 'em lovin' if they don't give you somethin'." And, "Cut 'em off if they piss you off."

Tom McQuade booked Madame Fortuno for Saturday night, June 8, 1940 at The Hotel Onondaga but he didn't know why he had done it. She believed in Christian Science and the audience would be doctors. She was part Negro and there wasn't a single person of color on the faculty or in the student body. She was a woman, there wasn't a female on the faculty and there were only two woman students in the entire medical school. She wouldn't use his script. She refused to embarrass anybody. She would deprive The Colonic of its retaliatory purpose. Yet, he booked her.

Maybe it was because of her alluring picture in the newspaper or her sultry voice on the telephone. Maybe she was just another challenge, like the foster homes, the streets of Pittsburgh, the wheelbarrows of cement, night school, organic chemistry and anatomy. Whatever the reason, he wanted to find out what it was.

Rejectionology

When I first started writing seriously, the sight of a returned SASE in the morning mail would flutter my stomach, aerate my brain and drive my self-esteem into a remote gulag for hours, sometimes even days. Time and again, I whined, pouted, cursed editors, secreted the rebuffs and even told friends "I only write for myself and not for publication." Right.

In those days, even a politely-worded rejection slip could cut like a chain saw. For example, whenever I got one of those bland, thank-you-very-much-for-yoursubmission-but-it-is-not-quite-right-for-us cards, I felt the message was YOUR MANUSCRIPT BEFOULED OUR SLUSH PILE! If an editor personalized the rejection and tried to be helpful with something like, "you got bogged down at page eleven," my interpretation was YOUR WORK IS NO DAMN GOOD AND NEITHER ARE YOU! And I won't even begin to describe my psycho-physiological response to the first, lay-it-on-the-line rejection slip that stabbed me with these words: "Please, no more submissions."

There was even one rejection that filled me with criminal compulsion. It happened after my then-agent had urged me to write a novel, after I had spent two years on the project, after he had gushed "what a book" and after he had submitted the manuscript to only one publisher. Then, without warning, he changed his mind and dropped the book, and suddenly the words "kill fee" took on a whole new meaning. Occasionally, I did get accepted, paid and published and that was all great fun. But rejection is lower than acceptance is high. And acceptance, especially when it is from a Big Time Publication, can make subsequent rejections even harder to endure.

For example, during a six-month period in 1991, *The New York Times Magazine* carried an "About Men" column I wrote; *The Wall Street Journal* published an essay of mine about a famous United States Supreme Court case; Harcourt Brace Jovanovich included that essay in a criminology textbook; *American Heritage* published a piece I had written about the Cold War; the *Wall Street Journal* essay landed me on "NBC Nightly News With Tom Brokaw;" agents telephoned from New York; and I even heard from a jasper in Hollywood who had "BIG" plans for my "About Men" column and who, to my shock, called me "darling" in our first telephone conversation. Soon, I was imagining book tours, opening nights, talk shows, a vegetarian lunch with Annie Dillard, schooners of Lone Star with Larry McMurtry, and straight shots of Rebel Yell with John Grisham.

But just after takeoff, my writing career crashed. No more "NBC Nightly News", *New York Times, Wall Street Journal, American Heritage,* literary agents, Hollywood slick-talkers, or fatuous daydreams, only an uncresting flood of rejection slips. Even with my fancy new credits, I couldn't sell anything to anybody, not even to one of those under-a-thousand-circulation quarterlies that "pay" with four extra copies of a single issue. Deflated by reality and dashed by fantasy, I felt the humiliation of hitting home runs in New York and then striking out in East Dubuque.

To make matters more complicated, my torments shifted away from rejection and settled on my vulnerability to it. Over and over, I gored myself for allowing returned manuscripts to trouble me in the first place. After all, I was a grown man. My livelihood didn't depend on writing. As a trial lawyer, I was hardened to bad verdicts. As a husband, I had survived divorce. So what in the world was wrong with me? Wasn't writing without publishing enough? Should I quit? If not, how should I cope? What should I do?

Eventually, the answers came when I understood what manuscript rejection is, what it isn't, who else had endured it, how most writers had coped, how a few hadn't, what helped, what didn't and, more than anything else, how almost everybody adjusts after getting rebuffed a few gazillion times. But this wisdom didn't come fast or easy as I had to suffer, research, and study hundreds of case histories. Now, at the end of that process, I am a self-proclaimed "rejectionologist" and my findings are as follows:

1. **What Is Rejection?** Narrowly defined, rejection is a decision made against purchasing or publishing a manuscript. That decision can be thoughtful (every word is read) or mindless (nothing is read). It can be objective (too short) or subjective (wrong tone). The decision-maker can be an experienced editor, a nineteen-year-old "reader," or a faceless administrative policy that filters out pre-designated categories of material. When analyzed properly, manuscript rejection never warrants despair, surrender or creative immobility.

2. **The Wrong Publication Rejection.** In a nanosecond, *People Magazine* would reject Hamlet but that wouldn't be an aspersion against the play or William Shakespeare. Similarly, a Nobel Laureate's article on ozone depletion would be rejected by *Scientific American* if it had just run a piece on that same topic. This kind of rejection implies nothing about the writer's talent and nothing about the manuscript's worthiness, only that it was sent to the incorrect magazine or publishing house.

3. **The Wrong Approach Rejection.** More apt to hurt are those rejections that are based on pace, mood, structure, or style. Yet, even these more subjective judgments do not justify razor blades on the wrist or word processors in the pond. Indeed, a case in point is this very article which *Writer's Digest* originally rejected because it did not, as the editor explained, "teach, instruct and/or inspire." So I re-wrote it and tried again.

4. **Rejection Should Hurt.** No matter how experienced or mature, writers will always feel some pain from rejection and that is how it should be. Writers cannot be indifferent to their work or what happens to it. Good writing always involves passion and passion is never blunted without pain.

5. **React In The Affirmative.** Always do something affirmative about rejection, just as I did with this essay. Rejections for writers should be like grains of sand for oysters.

6. Persist. The two most important, "oysterly" things to do are keep on writing and keep on submitting, no matter what. It took 21 rejections before *Newsweek* purchased an essay of mine for its "My Turn" column. In 1991, I wrote a Christmas story which was rejected by thirty-one consecutive publications, including *Phoenix Magazine.* Without changing a word, I sent the story back to *Phoenix Magazine* three years later and they published it in December, 1994. *The Chicago Tribune Magazine* ran it in December 1995 and *The Cleveland Plain Dealer Magazine* ran it again in December 1996.

7. Publication Is Not Everything. Even if *Phoenix Magazine* and *The Chicago Tribune Magazine* and *The Cleveland Plain Dealer* had not run my Christmas story, it was still as good before publication as it was afterwards and I learned a lot from writing it, especially about myself. In fact, I have file drawers full of unpublished manuscripts that helped me grow, learn and improve as a writer and as a person. As the British might say, not a bad result, that.

8. There Are Coping Techniques. One of the best compilations of practical tips for the rejected writer can be found in Scott Edelstein's *Writer's Book of Checklists* (Writer's Digest Books, 1991). Of Mr. Edelstein's twenty-one recommendations, there are two that work best for me. First, have so many manuscripts pending that the rejection of one is relatively inconsequential. Second, on the theory that you should always get back on the horse that threw you, send a rejected manuscript out to a different publication the same day that the returned SASE arrived.

9. Study Historical Rejections. The fastest way to adjust to rejection is to understand that all human beings get rejected, even those who are famous, successful and seemingly blessed. Company loves misery and so it is therapeutic to read John White's breezy *Rejection* (Addison-Wesley, 1982) and to learn about the rejections endured by Beethoven, Michelangelo, The Muppets, Abraham Lincoln, Stravinsky, Van Gough, Napoleon, Thomas Edison, Herman Melville, Thoreau, and hundreds of others. For more anecdotes and quotations about literary rejection, read James Charlton's classic *The Writer's Quotation Book* (Pushcart, 1991); Andre Bernard's fun *Rotten Rejections* (Pushcart, 1990); Sophy Burnham's soothing *For Writers Only* (Ballantine Books, 1994); and Kathleen Krull's businesslike *12 Keys To Writing Books That Sell* (Writer's Digest Books, 1989).

10. **Learn From The Victims.** Whenever a rejection starts to seriously bother me, I take it as a warning sign and think of John Kennedy Toole who wrote a comic novel about life in New Orleans called *A Confederacy of Dunces* (Louisiana State University Press, 1980). It was so relentlessly rejected that he committed suicide. After his death, his mother found a publisher and the book later won the Pulitzer Prize.

11. **Laugh At The Mistaken.** In rejecting Pearl Buck's *The Good Earth*, an editor wrote that "the American public is not interested in anything on China." In 1947, Thor Heyerdahl's *Kon Tiki* was returned by a young editor named William Styron who thought it was "a long, solemn and tedious Pacific voyage." Tony Hillerman was told, when his *The Blessing Way* was rejected, to "get rid of all that Indian stuff." About George Orwell's *Animal Farm*, one editor wrote that "it is impossible to sell animal stories in the U.S.A." Supposedly, Dr. Seuss's books were "too different" to sell. And proving that unknown writers have no chance even if they do great work, a freelancer named Chuck Ross typed up the first twenty-one pages of Jerzy Kosinski's *Steps*, which had already won the National Book Award; Ross then submitted those typed pages in 1975 to multiple publishers under the name of "Erik Demos;" and each publisher summarily rejected the manuscript with form letters. In 1977, Ross made his experiment even more dramatic; he typed every page of *Steps*; he sent off the typed manuscript again under the name "Erik Demos;" and each publisher rejected this award-winning book, even Random House which had published *Steps* in the first place.

12. **Cheer For The Persistent.** William Saroyan had a pile of rejection slips thirty-one inches high, maybe seven thousand in all, before he got his first

acceptance and went on to become one of America's most distinguished authors. Robert Persig was rejected one hundred and twenty times before *Zen and the Art of Motorcycle Maintenance* was accepted and became a best seller. Beatrix Potter gave up and self-published her timeless Peter Rabbit stories. Poet e e cummings, after being rejected so often that his mother had to publish his book, wrote the dedication in such a retaliatory way that he even used capital letters — "No thanks to: Farrar & Rinehart, Simon & Schuster, Coward-McCann, Limited Editions, Harcourt, Brace, Random House, Equinox Press, Smith & Haas, Viking Press, Knopf, Dutton, Harper's, Scribners, Covici, Friede."

13. If All Else Fails. In Paul Dixon's *The Official Rules* (Delacorte Press, 1978), there is a recommendation that I guarantee, if followed, will lessen the relative impact of a rejected manuscript. Just do this: eat a live toad for breakfast first thing in the morning and nothing worse will happen to you for the rest of the day.

CHAPTER FIVE

Clients, Causes and Cases

FREEDOM OF SPEECH, FREEDOM OF RELIGION AND THE RIGHT TO REMAIN SILENT

Representing The Hare Krishna in City Court

Representing My Wife In the United States Supreme Court

My Client, Ernesto Miranda

You Have The Right To Remain Silent

The Feds Bug Worship Services

Post 9-11 Freedom and Security

Peter Baird

Representing The Hare Krishna
In City Court

Poorly janitored, windowless, and illuminated by a grimy florescence, the Phoenix City Magistrate's Court handles the petty criminal offenses from downtown business and inner city squalor. In the late 1960's, arraignments were held every Tuesday morning for defendants charged during the preceding week with sex offenses or, as the florid bailiff put it, "with anything weird."

Walking down a hall littered with cigarette butts and filled with cops, dirty-shirt lawyers, and unsmiling litigants, my clients and I approached the door to courtroom number two and looked at the posted docket sheet. Evidently, it was going to be a typical Tuesday in Magistrate's Court because the schedule listed charges of prostitution (which veterans called "hooking"), indecent exposure ("flag-waving") and disturbing-the-peace-by-offensive conduct, which is a euphemism for public urination ("DP-by-PeePee").

My clients were named at the bottom of the docket sheet and would be the last defendants to step up before Judge Benjamin Salt and enter a plea. The charge against them was "criminal trespass by loitering."

According to prosecutors, my four clients — all members of the International Society For Krishna Consciousness or ISKCON — had trespassed at Park Central, which, back then, was a thriving, privately-owned shopping center. Heads shaved except for tufts in back, bodies clad in saffron robes and foreheads painted with clay markings, the Hare Krishnas had encamped in a busy mall intersection, clanged small hand cymbals, beat on a drum, danced about and endlessly chanted, "Hare Krishna, Hare Krishna, Krishna Krishna, Krishna Hare, Hare Hare, Hare Rama, Rama Rama, Hare Hare."

Vexed, mall security officers demanded evacuation; the Hare Krishnas responded with more clanging and chanting; and the police arrived to make arrests. The Hare Krishnas' "loitering" was, according to the jargon in the criminal complaint, "inconsistent with the mall's express and implied invitation to engage in commerce."

Yet, as my vacant-eyed clients saw things, they had a "spiritual right" to be there and to spread "holy oneness." After all, they had not blocked foot-traffic and they had only hawked an evangelistic tract, *Back to Godhead,* that no mall merchant carried in inventory. They were pursuing their religious beliefs, not putting on a "freak show" as mall management had alleged. And lastly, their clangings and chantings were an artistic improvement over the mall's Muzak.

Upon entering the courtroom, my colorful entourage immediately drew stares from the sex offenders, derelicts and everyone else present. As the five of us took our seats and all eyes riveted on us, I realized that my first mistake had been in loosely offering to do "any" free speech case for the Arizona Civil Liberties Union.

Too old to be a 1960's radical but too young to be a 1950's reactionary, I recently had graduated from Stanford Law School and had joined Lewis and Roca, a large Phoenix law firm. High-minded and full of myself, I entertained ambitions of handling "high-profile" "impact cases," preferably for professors, priests, rabbis, or ministers who opposed the Vietnam War. Not for a second did I imagine myself slumming in Magistrate's Court with a group of young men who looked like former pot heads and who were so deviant that even trench-coated exhibitionists looked down on them and, at the same time, me.

Ignoring the looks that were glued to us, I pored over the legal treaties I had brought with me and searched intensely for a loophole. Somehow, I had to end this mortifying case, avoid any more courtroom snickers and silence all the jokers back at the office.

Deep into the law books, I was jarred from my concentration by the judge's calling out my name, probably for the second or third time: "Mr. Baird, would you please approach the bench? Rattled, I quickly approached Judge Benjamin Salt, a kindly, bespectacled, round-faced man who later, after years of adjudicating drunks and vice, would take his own life in despair.

"Come closer, Mr. Baird," Judge Salt directed, leaning toward me. "What are your clients doing?," he asked. "Well, your honor, they're waiting to plead not guilty to —," I started to say but was abruptly cut off by the Judge. "I know why they are here but what in the hell are they doing?"

It was then that I turned around and looked out onto the courtroom at what Judge Salt was seeing from his bench: four loony-looking young men with their eyes shut vigorously moving their right hands in the crotch area of their robes. "My god, Mr. Baird, they are playing with themselves in my courtroom," Judge Salt hissed, loud enough for almost everyone to hear except for my own clients who were in another, more transcendental place at the moment.

"Holy Christ," I mumbled and, in four giant steps, was back to where my clients were seated, meditating and doing something in their nether regions. Shaking the nearest one by the shoulder and awakening them all from their collective trance, I tried to explain the situation in low tones, using euphemisms like "fooling around" and "privates." But either they couldn't hear or didn't understand because they kept asking me, with puzzled expressions, to "say again" and "please explain." Meanwhile, the pressure mounted, all courtroom business stopped and the judge fidgeted impatiently.

After my whispered sputters failed to convey the message, I finally spoke up, abandoned all indirection and, to the criminal delight of the sex offenders and immense entertainment of everyone else, blurted out the "m" word.

According to what my clients told me later, they had been meditating and their hands had been innocently handling prayer beads in little lap bags. But, in the end, it didn't matter where their hands had been because

I eventually found a loophole. In turn, the prosecutor dropped all charges but evened the score with a parting shot about the similarity between my legal arguments and my clients' manipulations.

A few weeks after the case was dismissed, the receptionist called me in my office and announced that there were "some very strange people here to see you." Without an appointment, my four Hare Krishnas had appeared in our lobby and were attracting stupefied looks from waiting clients and passing secretaries. As I approached, they greeted me with Ghandi-like gestures.

"We wanted to thank you for what you did for us," the eldest said, as he handed me a tin foil package the size of a football and the weight of a small anvil. "it is our ceremonial bread," he explained and then emphasized how all four of them had made the bread "with our own hands." Giving me only a moment to say something awkwardly polite, they quickly took their leave and the last I heard from them was the soft tinkle of a hand cymbal just as the elevator doors closed.

At home that night, I stared at the dense, grainy gift and wondered whether I was obliged to eat any of it, a piece of crust perhaps or maybe a few crumbs. I was relieved to have the case over and genuinely touched by their gesture. Still, I decided against even a nibble. After wrapping the ceremonial bread back up in the tin foil, I lugged the package outside and dropped it into the trash can with a leaden thud.

After all, I never was sure about that prayer bead story.

Representing My Wife In
The United States Supreme Court

Authorized by an Act of Congress in 1928, an architect named Cass
Gilbert designed the United States Supreme Court Building in Washington,
D.C. in a classical Greek style to symbolize not only "the national ideal of
justice in the highest sphere" but also a "co-equal, independent branch of
the United States Government." On the morning of December 8, 1969, our
taxicab stopped at the main entrance and we saw through the backseat
window what the architect had created: a wide oval plaza; long sweeping
steps; a portico with massive Corinthian columns; and the words "EQUAL
JUSTICE UNDER LAW" inscribed on the sculptured pediment.

Although my hands were sweating as much as my kidneys were pumping, I climbed out of the cab, paid off the driver and trudged the stairs with
my wife, briefcase and butterflies. I was 28-years old; I had only practiced
law for three years; and my professional experience had been so humdrum
that I sometimes encountered judges who had not even gone to law school.
Yet, there I was: walking through the bronze doors, entering the Great Hall,
and heading for an appearance before the nation's highest court.

Within the hour, I was scheduled to present the controversial case of
Sara Baird, Petitioner, v. State Bar of Arizona, Respondent, No. 1079, to the
Supreme Court. Sara was my wife and the issues involved loyalty, commu-
nism, freedom of belief, the First Amendment, and the practice of law.

Sara had graduated from Colorado College and Stanford University Law
School and had been number one on the bar examination. Nevertheless, the
Arizona State Bar Committee on Examinations and Admissions refused to
license her as a lawyer. Later, on January 14, 1969, the Arizona Supreme
Court upheld her exclusion and ruled for the State Bar Committee.

After losing at the Arizona Supreme Court, we took Sara's case to the United States Supreme Court by filing a "petition for writ of certiorari." On April 7, 1969, with Chief Justice Earl Warren presiding, the Court accepted Sara's case for review and set it for hearing, or "oral argument," on December 8, 1969. Since thousands of cases are presented to the Supreme Court each year and only about 150 are accepted for hearing, it was a statistical miracle that she had made it this far.

On her application form to become an Arizona lawyer, Sara had refused to answer question number 27 which asked: "Are you now or have you ever been a member of the Communist Party or any organization that advocates overthrow of the United States Government by force or violence?" Significantly, the Committee's purpose for asking about the Communist Party was to "trigger" further inquiries into an applicant's "beliefs" and "views."

If Sara had answered "yes" to question 27 and if she had admitted membership in the Communist Party, then the Committee promised to conduct an interrogation into her "beliefs" about revolution and the overthrow of the United States Government. If the men on the Committee were not comfortable with her "beliefs," then, as they were fond of saying, "we would want no part of her."

Despite Sara's refusal to answer question 27, she affirmatively wanted to take the lawyer's oath of office, which is a pledge to support the Constitution by one's conduct and which is approved by example in Articles II and V of the Constitution. In addition, she had already told the Committee, in response to another question, the names of all groups that she had belonged to since age 16. These were the "Church Choir; Girl Scouts; Girls Athletic Association; Young Republicans; Young Democrats; Stanford Law Association; Law School Civil Rights Research Council." Still, the Committee demanded to know specifically whether she had ever belonged to the Communist Party and, if so, what her views were on the subject of revolution.

As Sara and I looked for the Clerk's office where we were supposed to check in, we were not thinking about the long history behind this battle between the government, which wanted information about an individual's loyalty, and the citizen, who refused to give it. Yet, in a distant sense, Sara's case started in the Sixteenth Century when Henry VIII required his subjects to take "test oaths" that were directed at their beliefs. Those oaths were designed to coerce their loyalty to the Act of Succession and Henry's marriage to Anne Boleyn; they led to the execution of Sir Thomas More, among others, and established a precedent followed by Elizabeth I, the Stuarts and, eventually, by the federal, state, and municipal governments in the United States.

In this country, Alexander Hamilton defended a Royalist who had been victimized by a test oath in the Revolutionary Period. After the Civil War, the Supreme Court struck down various loyalty oaths that had prevented former Confederate officials from practicing law or acting as clergymen. By the mid-Twentieth Century, when Senator Joseph McCarthy and the House Un-American Activities Committee were on the loose, a profusion of loyalty oaths was promulgated as lawyers, teachers, professors, union officers, government employees, and political candidates had to disclose any membership in the Communist Party and affirm their loyalty as a precondition to licensing or employment. Indeed, the very question Sara refused to answer had been drafted into the Arizona Bar application following the decision of the American Bar Association, at its convention in 1950, to apply test oaths to all lawyers.

After waiting in the Counsel Room, staring blankly at the portraits of bearded Justices and worrying about a tongue that stuck to the roof of my mouth as if by velcro, I was summoned into the Court's Chambers where the oral argument would take place. This magnificent hearing room, with its columned visitor's gallery, counsel tables, and elevated mahogany bench for the Justices, had been the site of some of America's judicial worst and best. It was here, for example, that the Court disgraced itself in 1944 by the approval of mass internment for Japanese-Americans in the *Korematsu* case. This was also the place, ten years later, where the Court elevated the meaning of "equal protection" and banned the segregation of public schools in *Brown v. Board of Education.*

As I fidgeted at the counsel table, I looked up at nine, empty, high-backed chairs behind the bench. To the left sat the Clerk who administers the Court's docket. To the right sat the Marshall, who acts as timekeeper and who operates the white and red lights that signal when to stand up behind the lectern and speak and when to shut up and sit down.

With Sara seated behind me and two colleagues with me at the counsel table, I waited for the Justices to appear. Somehow, despite my inexperience and nerves, I had to convince the Court that Sara's refusal to answer the question was not an act of either petty obstructionism or left-wing guilt but rather was a serious, principled, and courageous stand that warranted First Amendment protection. Having been victimized by a loyalty crusade in Washington, D.C., some six years earlier, Sara knew from bitter personal experience just how pernicious these witch-hunts could be.

In 1963, after graduating from Colorado College, Sara worked for the World Bank and was under the aegis of the United States Civil Service Commission. Suddenly, without notice or explanation, she lost her security clearance. After she was forced to hire a lawyer and fight an administrative battle, she was fully reinstated and eventually told the "reason" for losing her security clearance.

It seems that Sara had been seen with a young man who, in turn, had been seen at a meeting of the W.E.B. DuBois Society, which was named after the co-founder of what became the NAACP. Once cleared, Sara quit her job at the World Bank, enrolled in Stanford Law School, worked in Mississippi for civil rights, established a legal services office for the Zuni Indians in New Mexico, and moved to Arizona where she passed the bar examination with, as the Committee grudgingly admitted, "flying colors." She steadfastly refused to take the oath of office and swear to uphold the Constitution while, at the same time, co-operating in the degradation of the First Amendment by answering question 27.

"Oyez, Oyez, Oyez," the Marshall said in a loud voice and we stood as the Justices filed in and took their seats. The Chief Justice was Warren Burger whom President Nixon had recently appointed to take the seat vacated by the now-retired Earl Warren. Flanking the Chief Justice in order of seniority were the Associate Justices Hugo L. Black, William O. Douglas, John M. Harlan, William J. Brennan, Jr., Potter Stewart, Byron R. White, and Thurgood Marshall. The Court was short one Justice because Abe Fortas had recently resigned in a cloud of scandal and the Democratically-controlled Senate had rejected Nixon's replacement nominee, Clement Haynsworth, only a few days earlier on November 21, 1969. Not until the Senate later rejected Nixon's second nominee, Harold Carswell, in April 1970 and approved the President's third choice, Harry Blackmun, in May 1970, was Fortas' seat finally filled.

Counting votes, we expected Black, Douglas, Brennan and Marshall to be with us and Harlan, Stewart, White and Burger to be against us. In 1961, when the last lawyer's loyalty oath cases came before the Court, one bar applicant from Illinois and another from California lost by narrow margins and in a welter of sharply-worded opinions and dissents. Unfortunately, Sara's case had not reached the Supreme Court a year earlier when Warren and Fortas were still there and when a majority that year had declared a teacher's loyalty oath from Arizona to be unconstitutional. During the past year, much had changed; realistically, Sara's prospects were not good.

"Mr. Baird, you may proceed," the Chief Justice said and the white light flashed on. Almost immediately, the conservative Justices broke into my canned presentation with dozens of questions that sometimes rained down simultaneously. Why should a communist be a lawyer? What groups had Sara really belonged to? If a lawyer actually believed in revolution, wouldn't she foment rebellion? Should police officers be asked if they were communists? What was wrong with the government asking Bar applicants their political beliefs?

By far, the most dyspeptic questioner was Chief Justice Burger who thought I was saying that "there is a constitutional right to overthrow the government by force and violence." Indeed, we did not expect the Chief Justice to be hospitable because he had tried, just a few weeks earlier, to prevent me from arguing Sara's case. Since I lacked the necessary years of practice to be automatically permitted to appear at the Court, I had petitioned the Chief Justice for special permission, which he refused. At Sara's insistence, we then appealed his decision to the entire Court, which reversed him, granted me permission and, probably, got me off on the wrong foot with Chief Justice Burger.

Flustered, I tried to explain, over and over, that lawyers should be judged by their conduct, character, and professional competence, but not by their personal, political, or religious beliefs, which were constitutionally protected from governmental inquiry by the First Amendment. In support of Sara's position, we relied on some of the most eloquent words ever written by the United States Supreme Court. There was, for example, the famous flag salute case, *West Virginia State Board of Education v. Barnett,* in which Justice Jackson wrote: "If there is any fixed star in our constitutional constellation, it is that no official, high or petty, can prescribe what shall be orthodox in politics, nationalism, religion or other matters of opinion or for citizens to confess by word or act their faith therein." There was also *Schneiderman v. United States,* where Justice Murphy said that, "The Constitutional Fathers, fresh from a revolution, did not forge a political straight jacket for generations to come. Instead they wrote the First Amendment guaranteeing freedom of thought."

As the pounding from the Court's conservatives continued, I lost my nervousness, patience and judgment all at the same time. Exasperated, I blurted that, if Sara were excluded from the practice of law because of unacceptable beliefs, then President Nixon should be disbarred for "believing" in an unconstitutional war in Vietnam that Congress had never declared.

The Justices were stunned, flabbergasted. How could any lawyer, even someone callow and brash, tell the United States Supreme Court that Richard M. Nixon, the President of the United States, should be disbarred? After the words came out of my mouth, the Courtroom fell into a strained, awkward, even horrified silence. Soon, to everyone's relief, the red light came on and I sat down, still brimming with adrenaline and poor judgment.

Momentarily, the white light illuminated and the lawyer for the Arizona State Bar, Mark Wilmer, stood up behind the lectern and started to explain why the Committee was entitled to know Sara's associations, views, and beliefs. Wilmer was tall, distinguished, experienced and the Senior Dean of the Arizona Trial Bar. Roughly the same age as some of the Justices, Wilmer addressed them as if they were his own peers discussing constitutional truisms at a downtown men's club.

"Whether we use the word 'belief,' the word 'view,' or whatever word we use, we are concerned with one thing," Wilmer said in his forceful yet *entre nous* style. "If Mrs. Baird *believes* in the sense that she would actively advocate and assist and advance the overthrow of the government of the United States in the State of Arizona by force and violence, well, we want no part of her." He elaborated: "We have admitted people [to the Arizona Bar] that in their younger days have committed burglary, statutory rape, what have you." However, "If Mrs. Baird says, 'I propose to walk up and down the streets after I am admitted as a lawyer, proclaiming to the world that I, a lawyer, believe we should change the form of government by force,'" then Wilmer repeated his favorite phrase: "we want no part of her." After a few polite questions and some *ex cathedra* answers, the red light went on and our stately opponent sat down, confident of victory.

Back home in Phoenix, I pored over the transcripts of the hearing and listened to friends tell me what an "idiot" and a "knucklehead" I had been for suggesting that President Nixon be disbarred. One colleague even quipped that I, not Nixon, should be the one disbarred for my incompetence in raising the President's disbarment with four Republican Justices and, especially, with Warren Burger whom Nixon had just appointed to be Chief Justice. Knowing my critics were right, all I could do was wait with Sara for a decision that never came.

In June 1970, we received a letter from the Clerk of the Court who informed us that there would not be a decision and that we should return to Washington in October 1970 for another argument. By then, President Nixon's newly-confirmed nominee, Harry Blackmun, would be on board and there would be a full nine-member Court. It did not take a constitutional scholar to figure out that there was a four-to-four deadlock. This meant, as a practical matter, that Justice Blackmun would decide the case.

"Oyez, Oyez, Oyez," came the now-familiar incantation from the Marshall and all nine Justices took their seats on the afternoon of October 14, 1970. Even though Justice Blackmun would later write the majority opinion in the abortion rights case of *Roe v. Wade* and be considered a judicial "liberal," he and the Chief Justice were, in those days, called "the Minnesota Twins" because they were both from Minnesota, close friends, conservative, and voted alike on myriad cases. Eventually, these two "twins" would be separated but not until after the decision in Sara's case.

Even before we returned to Washington, I vowed not to again mention the disbarment of President Nixon who, after all, had just placed Justice Blackmun, the swing vote, on the Court. Still, I had to neutralize the conservative Justices' revulsion to communism and somehow show that a lawyer could just as easily harbor thoughts of fascism. If I could demonstrate how selective the Committee had been in singling out left-wing beliefs rather than right-wing views, then maybe the conservatives, especially Justice Blackmun, could better appreciate why all political beliefs are protected by the First Amendment.

The white light came on and I quickly posed this hypothetical: "Take the ardent, hard-core racist who, in his mind disbelieves in the equal protection clause; he disbelieves in *Brown v. Board of Education*; and he believes in as many venal thoughts as he possibly can." I went on: "That man has the right to practice law just as much as the person who has an abhorrent left-wing belief because you judge a man by his conduct."

Unlike our earlier oral argument in December 1969 when the conservative Justices lacerated me with non-stop questions, this time they only asked a few questions and were remarkably polite. Maybe they did not want to provoke me into again calling for Nixon's disbarment. More likely, they had already made up their minds. The red light flashed on, my 30 minutes were over, and I sat down.

As before, Wilmer authoritatively stepped up to the lectern, saw the white light and resumed talking to his peers. Just then, Justice Black, who had been a First Amendment champion on the Court for decades and who had been largely silent during the first argument, exploded with a series of piercing questions. With Justice Black on the offensive and the other Justices mute, Wilmer conceded that the Committee had looked but could not find anything subversive about Sara. As he explained, "Nothing else [except for her refusal to answer question 27] in the files indicated that there was anything else wrong with this lady, that she had any bad background, that she belonged to any organizations that were wrong or anything else."

Under continued pressure from Justice Black, Wilmer also admitted that question 27 did not on its face directly call for the disclosure of any personal or political beliefs. However, a "wrong answer" to question 27 — that Sara belonged to the Communist Party — would "trigger" an interrogation by the Committee into Sara's "feelings" and "beliefs." According to Wilmer: "The entire purpose of that question — if the answer is yes — is to then interrogate the applicant as to what in fact are your present *feelings* and *beliefs* and *intentions* with respect to the overthrow of the government by violence. That is intended to trigger the Committee." Justice Black seemed pleased with that answer, sat back in his chair and let our opponent wrap up his argument.

In closing, Wilmer asked the Court to "balance" the competing interests at stake as he saw them. On the one hand, he said, there was a "little, old, tiny answer" that Sara refused to give. On the other hand, there was the "overthrow of the government by force and violence" that the Committee sought to avert. If those two, obviously unequal interests were "balanced," then the preservation of the Republic vastly outweighed Sara's First Amendment rights.

Just then, the red light went on, Wilmer sat down, and the Chief Justice declared that, "The case is submitted." This time, he was right.

On February 23, 1971, Justice Black wrote the Court's majority opinion, reversed the Arizona Supreme Court and explicitly ordered that Sara Baird be admitted to the practice of law. In his Opinion, Justice Black wrote that, "When a state attempts to make inquiries about a person's beliefs or associations, its power is limited by the First Amendment." Moreover, "broad and sweeping state inquiries under these protected areas, such as Arizona has engaged in here, discourage citizens from exercising rights protected by the Constitution." Justice Black went on to say that, "A state may not inquire about a man's views or associations solely for the purpose of withholding a right or benefit because of what he believes." "Indeed, we hold that views or beliefs are immune from Bar Association inquisitions designed to lay a foundation for barring an applicant from the practice of law. Clearly, Arizona has engaged in such questioning here." Finally, Justice Black concluded with this directive to the Committee and also to the Arizona Supreme Court:

> "The practice of law is not a matter of grace, but of right for one who is qualified by his learning and by his moral character. This record is wholly barren of one word, sentence, or paragraph that tends to show this lady is not morally and professionally fit to serve honorably and well as a member of the legal profession. It was error not to process her application and not to admit her to the Arizona Bar. The judgment of the Arizona Supreme Court is reversed and the case is remanded for further proceedings not inconsistent with this Opinion."

To everybody's surprise, newly-appointed Justice Blackmun did not "decide" the case at all. Instead, he dissented with his then "twin," Justice Burger, as well as with Justices White and Harlan. In his dissent, Justice Blackmun expressed incredulity that "a possessor of an academic degree from Colorado College and a possessor of a degree in law from Stanford University *refuses* to answer the 27th inquiry of the questionnaire."

Joining Justice Black to form the majority were Justices Douglas, Brennan, Marshall and, to our astonishment, Stewart, who must have changed his mind since the first argument, who must have been the tie-breaker, and who wrote a terse concurring Opinion. As Justice Stewart saw it, the Committee was trying to find out about "an applicant's beliefs" that were somehow "objectionable" and he concluded that "The First Amendment and the Fourteenth Amendment bar a state from acting against any person merely because of his beliefs."

On March 30, 1971, the Arizona Supreme Court complied with the mandate from the United States Supreme Court, held a special session, and swore in Sara Baird as a member of the State Bar of Arizona, with her young children watching. Since then, she has not attempted to overthrow the government by force or violence or by any other means. However, three years later, there was a postscript.

In its September 13, 1974 edition, the *Washington Post* carried an Associated Press story under this headline: "Nixon Resignation From California Bar Received by Court." According to the news article, former President Nixon had resigned in lieu of disbarment from the California State Bar, not for any beliefs or views, but because of his illegal conduct in obstructing the Watergate investigation.

Oyez, Oyez, Oyez.

My Client, Ernesto Miranda

In a distant sense, *Miranda v. Arizona*, 384 U.S. 436 (1966), started on the eve of the English Civil War, when a cantankerous young Puritan by the name of "Freeborn" John Lilburne was arrested in 1637, charged with the importation of heretical and seditious books into England and taken to the Star Chamber for one of its indelicate interrogations. For his refusal "to take a legal oath" and "to answer truly," Lilburne was whipped, pilloried, fined and imprisoned. Erwin N. Griswold, *The Fifth Amendment Today* (Harvard University Press, Cambridge, 1955). Four years later, the House of Commons declared his treatment illegal, the House of Lords indemnified him and the privilege against self-incrimination was born.

Even though he most certainly had never heard of John Lilburne, Ernesto Arturo Miranda was to become a remote, and perhaps most famous, beneficiary of what Lilburne had done over 300 years earlier. Born in Mesa, Arizona in 1941 as the fifth son of an immigrant house painter father from Sonora, Mexico, Miranda suffered significantly when, at the age of six, his mother died. After that, his early life became a succession of conflicts with his stepmother, truancies from Queen of Peace Grammar School, and steadily worsening disciplinary problems. *See generally* Baker, *Miranda* (Crime Law and Politics) (Antheneum, New York, 1985). An early watershed year for *Miranda* was 1954, when he finished his eighth and last year of formal education and when he was also convicted of his first serious crime. From that point on, he became the prototype of the practiced recidivist with one illegal act, arrest and conviction after another and with assorted incarcerations between 1957 and 1961 in Arizona, California, Texas, Tennessee and Ohio. During one period of freedom, he enlisted in the United States Army but, true to form, he was dishonorably discharged after going AWOL and after doing hard labor at the Post Stockade at Fort Campbell, Kentucky.

By 1962, Miranda was out of jail and back in the Phoenix area, working as a produce worker and living with a "common-law" wife named Twila Hoffman. A hard-luck case with two children by a man she could not afford to divorce, Twila cohabited with Miranda and gave birth to his daughter, Cleopatra. Five years later, to his rage and dismay, Twila would betray him when she testified for the State in his retrial after the United States Supreme Court decision.

Despite job, family and the appearance of momentary stability, Miranda could not break one of his worst and most dangerous habits — preying upon young women. According to the Phoenix police, Miranda repeatedly abducted, kidnapped, raped, and, occasionally, robbed an indeterminate number of young women. His *modus operandi* was so rigid and his cruising grounds were so limited that, in March 1963, his beat-up Packard was spotted and his license plates were read by a recent victim near the very site where she had been abducted just a week earlier. With a description of the car and a partial license plate number, detectives soon appeared at Miranda's door.

On March 13, 1963, Phoenix police officers Cooley and Young arrested Ernesto Miranda, took him to the station house and placed him in a lineup. The rape victim could not positively identify him, although she wanted to hear the sound of his voice. After the lineup, he asked the police officers how he had done and they dissembled, telling him that he had flunked and distinctly implying that there had been a positive identification.

Whether he was overwhelmed by the interrogation process or whether he believed the proverbial jig was up, Miranda confessed to the 1963 rape-kidnapping charge that would become, three years later, the landmark United States Supreme Court decision. He also owned up to a 1962 robbery-kidnapping charge that was not taken to the Supreme Court and that would surprise, vex and embarrass us. As would be important later,

Miranda's two confessions were virtually identical — made at the same time, in the same place, to the same officers and under the same circumstances.

After unburdening himself to Officers Cooley and Young, Miranda was taken to meet the rape victim so that she could hear the sound of his voice for possible identification purposes. Asked by the officers in her presence whether this was the victim, Miranda said, "that's the girl." As it happened, the sound of his voice was extremely useful because she was then able, right then and there, to identify him as the culprit, without doubt or further hesitation.

After this creative law enforcement work was over, Miranda then wrote his confessions down on some mimeographed police forms. At the top of each sheet, above the space for his self-incrimination, was the printed certification that the confessor makes ". . . this statement voluntarily and of my own free will, with no threats, coercion or promises of immunity and with full knowledge of my legal rights, understanding any statement I make may be used against me." Despite the boilerplate recitation that Miranda was confessing "with full knowledge of my legal rights," he was not informed, as most of the American legal community now knows, of his "full legal rights." Written in what writer Liva Baker aptly describes as a "spidery cursive hand," Miranda's famous rape and kidnapping confession, in its unexpurgated form, is as follows:

"Seen a girl walking up street stopped a little ahead of her got out of car walked towards her grabbed her by the arm and asked to get in the car. Got in car without force tied hands & ankles. Drove away for a few miles. Stopped asked to take clothes off. Did not, asked me to take her back home. I started to take clothes off her without any force, and with cooperation. Asked her to lay down and she did, could not get penis into vagina got about 1/2 (half) inch in. Told her to get clothes back on. Drove her home. I couldn't say I was sorry for what I had done. But asked her to say a prayer for me."

State v. Miranda, 98 Ariz. 18, 28, 401 P.2d 721 (1965).

Subsequently, Miranda was bound over for separate, back-to-back trials set down for June 1963 before Maricopa County Superior Court Judge Yale McFate on the robbery and rape charges. Assigned to the defense in each case was a 73-year-old lawyer by the name of Alvin Moore, who had, years before, obtained his law degree by correspondence from the LaSalle University School of Law in Chicago, who was paid $100 for each trial from county funds and who, despite his lack of criminal expertise, accepted this representation at the specific request of Judge McFate. Even doing his best, Moore could not contain his revulsion for Miranda and, in an amazing statement, told the jury, "You know, perhaps a doctor doesn't enjoy operating for locked bowels, but he has to."

No matter what his limitations or aversions might have been, Moore laid a foundation for what later became an historic Supreme Court decision. When the prosecutor offered Miranda's written confession in evidence with officer Cooley on the witness stand, Moore conducted the following *voir dire*:

MR. MOORE: Officer Cooley, in the taking of this statement, what did you say to the defendant to get him to make this statement?

A. I asked the defendant if he would tell us, write the same story that he had just told me, and he said the he would. Q. Did you warn him of his rights?

A. Yes, Sir, at the heading of the statement is a paragraph typed out, and I read this paragraph to him out loud . . . .

Q. But did you ever, before or during your conversation or before taking this statement, did you ever advise the defendant he was entitled to the services of an attorney?

A. When I read —

Q. Before he made any statement?

A. When I read the statement right there.

Q. I don't see in the statement that it says where he is entitled to the advise [sic] of an attorney before he made it.

A. No, Sir.

Q. It is not in that statement?

A. It doesn't say anything about an attorney. Would you like for me to read it?

Q. No, it will be an exhibit if it is admitted and the jury can read it, but you didn't tell him he could have an attorney.

State v. Miranda, 98 Ariz. 18, 27-28, 401 P.2d 721 (1965).

Moore was obviously thinking about *Gideon v. Wainwright,* 372 U.S. 369, (1963), which had been decided only five days after Miranda's confession. Presumably based upon it, Moore protested the use of Miranda's confession and said on the record, "We are objecting because the Supreme Court of the United States says a man is entitled to an attorney at the time of his arrest." Judge McFate overruled the objection, the confession was received in evidence and, not surprisingly, Miranda was convicted of rape and kidnapping. Indeed, the robbery case had already proceeded in a parallel fashion: the confession was introduced; an off-center objection was made; the objection was overruled; and Ernesto Miranda was convicted of yet another felony.

For the rape conviction, Judge McFate sentenced Miranda to 20 to 30 years. For the robbery conviction, the Judge stacked on an additional 20 to 25 year consecutive term. After his sentencing in June 1963, Miranda was taken to the Arizona State Prison in Florence, a bleak and forbidding place that cooks in summer temperatures as high as 115 degrees. When he began serving his time and working as a prison barber, Miranda was just another anonymous "con," but one relegated to second class prison society status because he was, after all, a "rape-o." In three years, all of that would change.

In the meantime, Moore appealed both convictions to the Arizona Supreme Court and filed his briefs in December, 1963. After that, while Miranda barbered in prison and Moore waited in Phoenix, these cases came to a virtual standstill in the Arizona appellate system. Eventually, some sixteen months later, in April, 1965, the Arizona Supreme Court affirmed both convictions in two separate decisions. In the rape opinion, *Miranda v. State*, 98 Ariz. 18, 36, 37, 401 P.2d 721 (1965), the court dealt squarely with the confession issue; found Moore's trial objections wanting; used the boilerplate recitations in the confession form as an indication that Miranda "understood his legal rights;" distinguished *Escobedo v. Illinois*, 378 U.S. 478 (1964); and concluded that "it was proper to admit the statement in evidence." In the robbery opinion, *Miranda v. State*, 98 Ariz. 11, 14, 401 P.2d 716 (1965), the court noted in passing that Miranda had "confessed to the robbery" but never addressed the legality or admissibility of that confession at all.

After their release in April, 1965, these two appellate decisions came to the attention of Robert J. Corcoran, who later became a Justice on the Arizona Supreme Court and who was looking then, on behalf of the ACLU, for an appropriate case which would allow the United States Supreme Court to formulate something more uniform and objective than the case-by-case standards laid down by *Escobedo*. A former criminal prosecutor himself, Corcoran knew well that confessions were often obtained from uneducated suspects who did not have the vaguest idea what their rights were.

In June, 1965, Corcoran called one of our partners, the late John J. Flynn, about taking on Miranda's cases. A former World War II combat Marine and former criminal prosecutor, Flynn was by then a legendary criminal defense lawyer who was as brilliant in the courtroom as he was feckless in law firm economics. With hardly a hesitation, Flynn agreed to take Miranda's cases. In turn, he enlisted the help of another partner, John P. Frank, a Supreme Court scholar and historian and Justice Hugo Black's former law clerk, who was keen for any constitutional battle, whether for a social pariah like Miranda or for a member of the corporate glitteratti. Over the philosophical objections of some and the monetary concerns of others, our firm formally accepted the *pro bono* representation of Ernesto A. Miranda, with Flynn and Frank leading some eager young lawyers.

One of the first decisions made was to take the rape case, but not the robbery case, to the Supreme Court. While Alvin Moore's objections to both confessions were far from perfect, his objection was better in the rape case than in the robbery case. Moreover, the Arizona Supreme Court had confronted the confession directly in its rape opinion but had made only a passing reference to the confession in the robbery opinion. Even if the robbery case were left behind, there would be no problem, Flynn and Frank reasoned, because if one confession was unconstitutional then surely the other one would be too. Or so it seemed at the time.

On June 13, 1966, Chief Justice Warren announced one of the most momentous decisions ever rendered by the United States Supreme Court, reversing the Arizona Supreme Court, overturning Miranda's rape conviction and holding that suspects in custody must be explicitly told of their constitutional rights before their statements made to police could be admissible. To our considerable surprise, the Court's decision was based on the fifth amendment. Like Alvin Moore, our firm had treated this case principally as a sixth amendment, right to-counsel problem and not as a fifth amendment, privilege against self-incrimination issue. However, regardless of grounds, our client had scored a great victory and had uncapped, at the same time, a gusher of publicity.

For a then-small Phoenix law firm, this was a moment of real exultation. Although the firm joyfully bathed and splashed in the limelight, there were, in retrospect, reasons for moderating our excited pride. For one thing, *Miranda* might have been so inevitable after *Escobedo v. Illinois*,

378 U.S. 478 (1964), that even a dentist could have handled the case and won. Moreover, the decision is called *Miranda* for the flukey reason that Miranda's petition was filed before those of appellants Vignera, Stewart and Westover, whose convictions also were reversed in the same opinion.

As it turned out, the party did not last long. Just seven days later, the law gods turned on us and *Johnson v. New Jersey,* 384 U.S. 719, 732 (1966), was decided. Again, Chief Justice Warren wrote for the Court but this time said, to our astonishment, "that *Escobedo* and *Miranda* . . . should not be applied retroactively." If the *Miranda* decision applied only to the future and not to the past, then *Miranda's* robbery conviction — the one that our newly-famous law firm did not appeal — would be untouched by *Miranda's* own Supreme Court decision and would stand as an unappealable finality. The situation was utterly bizarre: when Miranda simultaneously made two confessions on March 13, 1963 at the same time, at the same place, to the same officers and under identical circumstances, one was constitutional and the other was unconstitutional. Even though this had never happened before in the history of American constitutional law, this intriguing uniqueness did nothing to ease our post mortem pain.

Meanwhile, down at the Arizona State Prison, Ernie was barbering away, ecstatic about his victory in Washington, D.C., utterly delighted with all the publicity and remarkably forgiving about our prospectivity problem in the robbery case. Overnight, he was no longer just "another con" but a genuine hero among his prison peers who said admiringly, "Ernie doesn't confess." Yet, the inmate sloganeers had it all wrong because Ernie had in fact confessed. To complicate matters, he may have taken this "Ernie doesn't confess" business so literally himself that certain vital information was never divulged even to his own lawyers.

After putting in uncountable research hours on the prospectivity issue and after learning the hard way what *sui generis* really meant, we eventually filed a *habeas corpus* petition in federal district court. Based upon a contorted version of the law of the case principle, our thesis was that, when declaring Miranda's rape confession unconstitutional, the United States Supreme Court also invalidated Miranda's robbery confession without knowing it or saying it. At the hearing, John Flynn ignored virtually all of our awkward legal arcana and basically repeated the credo of all lawyers who lack solid legal authority: "Your Honor, it is just, plain wrong." To our redemptive relief, the court agreed and, because of the obvious identities between the two confessions, vacated Miranda's robbery conviction.

In February 1967, Miranda was retried for the rape and kidnapping charge before a sequestered jury. Although the trial lasted for eight days, only one-half day was spent before the jury with the balance of the time devoted to sorting out what was connected to the unlawful confession and what was not. No longer defended by a disapproving grandfather, Miranda was this time represented by the formidable John Flynn, who was made even more intimidating by the citations, motions and briefs from his energetic young associates. The prosecutor was the resourceful Robert Corbin, who later became the Arizona Attorney General and whose task was to convict Miranda without either the confession, which the United States Supreme Court had invalidated, or the rape victim's voice identification, which the trial court excluded as being "fruit" from a "tree" poisoned by the illegal confession.

Through prosecutorial good fortune, Twila Hoffman fortuitously surfaced to become the State's star witness and testimonial substitute for both the confession and the victim identification. It seems that, while Miranda was in prison, Twila had found another man, had given birth to another baby, and was not eager for Ernie's return. Over forceful but unsuccessful objections, she told the jury about a conversation she and Miranda had in jail the day after his arrest, back in March, 1963. According to her, he admitted raping the victim and, as if that were not enough, he even implored Twila to approach the victim and offer her his own felonious hand in marriage. With this incriminating and seemingly lunatic story in evidence, Miranda was convicted again of rape and kidnapping and returned for more time and more barbering at the Arizona State Prison.

Much later, in 1971, Miranda eventually was retried for the robbery and kidnapping charge. By then, John Mitchell had become the Attorney General of the United States and the "*Miranda* case" and the "*Miranda* warnings" had become so politically controversial that Miranda was tried under the alias, "Jose Gomez," which is a Spanish equivalent of John Doe. Even though Miranda's robbery confession was excluded from evidence because of the ruling in the *habeas corpus* case, the robbery victim had made a clear-cut identification of him back in 1963 and she repeated her unequivocal observation to the jury in 1971. To make matters worse for Miranda, one of the jurors became extremely suspicious about who this Jose Gomez really was and, evidently, was able to make a difference late in the deliberations.

After the verdict was read and the conviction was announced, the trial judge insisted that Jose Gomez tell the jury his real name. With his lawyers refusing to participate in this minor bit of gratuitous theater, Jose Gomez awkwardly introduced himself to the very people who had just convicted him. Confirming the necessity for the alias, the jury visibly and audibly reacted to the name "Miranda," which had been so widely publicized and much accursed during the "law and order" debates of those times.

The ultimate irony is that Miranda never served any less time as a result of his famous decision. Indeed, he may even have served more time because of the scrutiny the Arizona Parole Board gave to its most famous customer. After rejecting his applications on four successive occasions, the Board finally, on a split vote, paroled Miranda in December 1972. His freedom, however, was not to last. When police later found him with a loaded pistol and several amphetamines, Miranda was promptly returned, after an unsuccessful legal skirmish, to prison for more time and more barbering.

Eventually, after years of intermittent and extended confinements, Miranda was released from prison for the last time in March, 1975. Unable to work as a barber because his felonies made licensing impossible, he worked at a tire company and supplemented his income by selling autographed *Miranda* warning cards for between $1.50 and $2.00 each. Perhaps it was predictable, but he would not survive long "outside."

On January 31, 1976, Miranda participated in a card game at the La Amapola Bar in a seedy section of Phoenix called "the Deuce." Charges of cheating were exchanged and a violent fight broke out. After this melee was over, Miranda retired to the men's room to wash blood from his hands. Just as he emerged, two men attacked him. Whether the weapon was a lettuce knife as one report says or a linoleum knife as another account states, the brutal and fatal fact is that Ernesto Arturo Miranda was mortally wounded that evening, dead on arrival at Good Samaritan Hospital. He was 35 years old.

When police later arrested a Hispanic male for the murder, one of the first things they did was to take out a little, rectangular card and, in English and in Spanish, start reading the words, "You have the right to remain silent . . . ." Whether the police knew it or not, those words represented a venerable right, which began with the excesses of the Star Chamber in London; which developed during three turbulent centuries; which traveled across a vast ocean and nearly an entire continent; and which eventually reached the lives of some violent, social misfits at a squalid bar in Phoenix, Arizona.

"Freeborn" John would have been proud.

You Have The Right To Remain Silent

The *Miranda* warning. Civil libertarians have praised it, critics such as *The Wall Street Journal* have condemned it, and police officers recite it thousands of times a day.

It was the result of the Supreme Court's most famous criminal decision, made 25 years ago today. In its 5-to-4 decision in *Miranda v. Arizona*, perhaps its most famous criminal case, the court held that arrested suspects must be advised of their constitutional rights before their confessions to police could be presented at trial.

After laboring for years with subjective and variable criteria, the court in *Miranda* formulated objective and uniform standards and required that specific, constitutional information be read to persons in custody. Only when suspects understand their rights can they waive those rights. For years, critics have denounced *Miranda* for blocking confessions from un-warned suspects and for mandating that constitutional information be given to citizens when they need it most — upon their arrest. According to its detractors, *Miranda* undermines the criminal justice system because police investigations have been compromised, law enforcement has become more difficult, and dangerous criminals have gone unprosecuted or have been turned loose on a "technicality." Met head-on, these criticisms are wrong or are hugely exaggerated.

In almost every instance, *Miranda* does not affect methods of pre-arrest investigation and detection because the court's decision applies only to suspects in custody. For this reason, police need not read "*Miranda* warnings" to witnesses, third parties or even suspects themselves until they are actually under arrest. *Miranda* only crimps police activities when they conduct custodial interrogations.

Has *Miranda* made law enforcement more difficult? Of course it has. For 25 years, police have been forced to read constitutional rights to hundreds of thousands of suspects, without word games, lies, or qualifiers. If the arresting officers are not professional enough to read the *Miranda* warnings in the first place, and if the only evidence is unwarned suspect's confession, then the prosecutor's case will be stillborn. However:

- Reading suspects their rights is hardly more than a nettlesome inconvenience for police. And under the Constitution, it is supposed to be difficult to deprive citizens of their liberty.
- Unlike other constitutional protections such as trial by jury, *Miranda's* "burden" on the justice system can be shouldered quickly and inexpensively. It takes only seconds for trained officers to read *Miranda* warnings.
- All *Miranda* did was "constitutionalize" what the FBI had been doing for years before — read arrested suspects their rights. Surely the FBI would not have engaged in a practice that compromised effective law enforcement.
  As the Supreme Court ruled in 1971 in *Harris v. New York*, *Miranda* does not give suspects a license to lie. If police fail to warn a suspect properly and the suspect confesses, the police can then read the suspect a *Miranda* warning. If the suspect at that point changes his mind and denies the crime, the original confession can still be presented at trial to "impeach" or contradict the suspect's denial.
  But what about the principal law-and-order argument: that *Miranda* has permitted dangerous criminals to go free? Has this "judicially invented technicality" stifled the rate of confession, indictment and conviction? The realities are these:
- According to John Kaplan of the Stanford Law School in a November 1987 issue of the *American Bar Association Journal*, suspects confess just as easily when they are given their *Miranda*

warnings as when they are not. The more polite and professional the police, the more inclined suspects are to talk, explain or unburden themselves.

- Empirical studies bear Professor Kaplan out. In 1981, the Ohio State Law Journal reported the field research as demonstrated that *Miranda* has not significantly affected the number or rate of confessions to crimes "cleared" but not prosecuted.

- Once prosecutors have confessions in hand, remarkably few founder at trial. *Newsweek* reported in July 1988 that fewer than 1% of criminal cases are thrown out because of defective confessions. Of that 1%, only a fraction were voided because of noncompliance with *Miranda*. A 1983 study of 260 arrests for robbery in California found that no evidence at all was excluded on *Miranda* grounds. Another analysis of 2,804 cases in 38 U.S. attorneys' offices revealed that only 4.4% of defendants even filed motions to suppress their own confessions at trial.

- Given these studies and statistics, it is not surprising that the overwhelming bulk of informed opinion affirmatively favors *Miranda* or, at least, finds its impact to be neutral. Both former Justice Tom Clark, who dissented in *Miranda*, and former Chief Justice Warren Burger, whom President Nixon appointed to the Supreme Court, have expressed the view — in a 1989 issue of the University of Chicago Law Review — that *Miranda* has not had a negative impact on criminal prosecutions. And this acceptance is not restricted to lofty judges or cloistered academics.

- Perhaps the best example of how the *Miranda* decision did not turn loose the criminal population is Ernesto Miranda himself. After the Supreme Court reversed his conviction, Miranda was re-tried without his confession being presented in court and he was convicted again and re-sentenced, all without enjoying a single day of freedom. Indeed, because of the scrutiny the Arizona Parole Board gave its most famous petitioner, Miranda probably served more, not less, time in prison as a result of the Supreme Court's landmark ruling in his own case.

Miranda is anything but a mindless "technicality." Even if everything its critics said were true, *Miranda* would still make compelling, constitutional sense. It all comes down to this: The organized criminal, the educated, and the affluent are almost always aware of their constitutional guarantees when they confront the state in a criminal showdown, but there are literally millions of functionally illiterate, poor, and uneducated citizens who do not know what their rights are when the cuffs snap on, the pressure is applied or, as recently happened in Los Angeles, the night sticks strike. More than anything else, *Miranda v. Arizona* means that information about our Constitution is no longer rationed on the basis of wealth, experience, or education.

Happy Anniversary, *Miranda v. Arizona.*

Peter Baird

The Feds Bug Worship Services

And they watched him, and sent forth spies, which should feign themselves just men, that they might take hold of his words, that so they might deliver them unto the power and authority of the governor. *Luke* 20:20

At approximately 11:30 a.m. on October 1, 1984, undercover agent PHO-1-92 turned on his "body-bug" — a secret tape recording device — and called Sister Dottie Deger from a pay telephone somewhere in Phoenix. Posing as "Jose Morales," agent PHO-1-92 asked the nun about "the sanctuary thing" and was particularly interested in information about a well-publicized car caravan coming from Tucson and carrying a Salvadoran refugee family. With PHO-1-92 was another agent, PHO-I-98.

Untrained in law enforcement, PHO-1-92 and PHO-1-98 were working undercover for the Federal Immigration and Naturalization Service, or "INS," which gave them cash, electronic eavesdropping equipment and instructions. For much of 1984, the INS directed PHO-1-92 and PHO-1-98 to infiltrate, monitor, and sometimes tape record Catholic Masses, Presbyterian worship services, and Lutheran Bible study sessions in Nogales, Tucson and Phoenix, Arizona. In truth, PHO-1-92 was Solomon Graham and PHO-1-98 was Jesus Cruz.

Specifically, the INS wanted Graham and Cruz to gather information about alien smuggling operations allegedly being conducted by various religious groups. For this, they were ideally suited because both men had themselves illegally immigrated to the United States and each was a "coyote," as those who professionally transport "illegals" are called. Between 1978 and 1980, Cruz had moved illegal aliens 20 or 30 different times and charged up to $500 a trip. For his smuggling activities, Graham had been arrested three times, deported once, and convicted once; he had served time in a federal correctional facility; and, according to one court filing, Graham even had been involved with a prostitution ring at work camps for " illegals."

After the INS threatened both men with deportation, Cruz and Graham agreed to work undercover in something that the INS called "Operation Sojourner" after this passage in Leviticus 12:33-34: "When a stranger sojourns with you in your land, you shall do him no wrong." The name, Operation Sojourner, must have been a bureaucratic joke because the INS neither practiced nor preached *Leviticus.*

Operation Sojourner was formulated by the INS in March 1984 to infiltrate and then, as one internal document put it, "disband" something called the Sanctuary Movement — a loose, national coalition of individuals, churches and temples dedicated to temporarily relocating refugees from war-torn Central America to this country or to Canada. To the Reagan Administration, the Sanctuary Movement ran an illegal "underground railroad" for deportable "economic" refugees and was a festering public relations sore.

To the Sanctuary Movement, the Reagan Administration was supporting military regimes and death squads that drove thousands of Guatemalans and Salvadorans out of their countries and, north, into the United States. When undocumented Central Americans were arrested in this country, the INS classified them "economic" rather than "political" refugees and sent almost all of them back to their peril. In the Sanctuary Movement's view, Central Americans were being treated in a manner reminiscent of the boatloads of Jewish refugees whom America turned away and forced back into Nazi hands just prior to World War II.

Unaware that she was being tape recorded by the federal government, Sister Dottie told "Jose Morales" on the telephone that the Sanctuary Movement caravan, with the Salvadoran family, would stop at the Franciscan Renewal Center for a "potluck supper tonight." Afterwards, she explained, the procession would travel a few miles west, on Lincoln Drive, to the

Camelback Presbyterian Church for a 7:30 p.m. "ecumenical prayer service" to be conducted by "clergymen from different religions."

Sister Dottie went on to say that the Unitarian Church of Phoenix would host a breakfast the next morning and, after that, the group would caravan off to Albuquerque. Pleased about his call and expression of support, Sister Dottie asked "Jose Morales" if he would join the cavalcade and show his solidarity by putting a sign on his pick-up, reading "Caravan for Peace." "Jose" gushed with enthusiasm and promised to come to the potluck supper, attend the ecumenical prayer service, and even bring a friend.

At approximately 6:00 p.m. on October 1, 1984, Jesus Cruz and Solomon Graham appeared at the elegant, Spanish-style Franciscan Renewal Center, which is located in the wealthy Phoenix suburb called Paradise Valley and which is an oasis of Catholic liberalism in a conservative diocese and an even more conservative state. Before Cruz and Graham could settle in for the potluck dinner, they spotted someone who knew their real identities and so they immediately bolted, as Graham muttered into his body-bug, "for the fucking door."

Later, just after 7:30 p.m. that same evening, Cruz and Graham drove into the parking lot of the Camelback Presbyterian Church, where the ecumenical prayer service was starting. A few miles west of the Franciscan Renewal Center and also within an area of extravagant wealth, The Camelback Presbyterian Church overlooked the City of Phoenix, ministered principally to upscale Presbyterians and shared its facility with another congregation, Sunrise Presbyterian Church. After climbing out of their car, Cruz and Graham paused briefly to dictate a license plate number into the body-bug. "BRC619. . . Chevrolet, Arizona plate . . . Boy, Robert, Carlos 619," Graham told his microphone.

At the church door, Cruz and Graham took printed bulletins that described, in Spanish and English, the order of worship that would be conducted by Catholic, Presbyterian, Lutheran, and Unitarian clergy.

Once in the church sanctuary, Cruz and Graham fraudulently posed as worshipers and took their seats. Already, the congregants were singing the opening hymn: "Somos Un Pueblo" or "We Are a People."

Neither Cruz nor Graham had a warrant from a federal magistrate that would have permitted them to covertly attend these services or, in legal terms, to conduct a "search" of the sanctuary and to "seize" the worshipers' prayers, hymns, or Bible readings on tape. Two years later, the United States Justice Department lawyers would admit in federal court that nothing illegal occurred at this October 1, 1984 ecumenical service. Yet, according to the government lawyers, the INS did not need anything — a warrant, the suspicion of foul play or any reason at all — before it could send spies and tape recorders into "any" religious worship service "at any time."

As the October 1 ecumenical service progressed, Graham's sensitive bodybug recorded virtually everything: the invocation; the responsive reading; a spiritual dialogue; the prayer of confession; the assurance of pardon; Bible passages from Isaiah, Hebrews and the Psalms; a sermonized condemnation of the killings in Central America; "testimony" from the Salvadoran family about death and hardship in their homeland; and, finally, a reading from the very passage that gave Operation Sojourner its name. According to the transcript of the government's tape recording, an "unidentified male" read out loud the full text of *Leviticus* 19:33-34: "When a stranger sojourns with you in your land, you shall do him no wrong. The stranger who sojourns with you shall be to you as the native among you and you shall love him as yourself; for you were strangers in the land of Egypt; I am the Lord your God."

Near the end of the service when the collection plate headed their way, Cruz and Graham hurriedly left the sanctuary, walked straight to the men's room and, with body-bug still running, recorded themselves urinating. From there, they went back to the parking lot and Graham resumed dictating worshipers' license plate numbers into his hidden microphone. "BAH902 . . . CEJA67 . . . temporary plate 817-420," Graham said out loud.

Operation Sojourner and the October 1, 1984 tape recording did not remain secret for long. On January 14, 1985, the federal government indicted six-teen Sanctuary Movement workers — including two Catholic priests, three nuns, and one Presbyterian minister — for operating an illegal "underground railroad" and for "transporting, harboring and aiding and abetting the entry of illegal aliens into the United States." As the indictments were being announced, squads of INS agents swept barrio neighborhoods in Phoenix and Tucson, arresting Central Americans who had been seen at Catholic Masses, Lutheran Bible study sessions, or Presbyterian worship services monitored by Cruz and Graham.

The stunning revelation of government spies and body-bugs in religious services came out during the pre-trial hearings in the criminal case. It happened on May 23, 1985, when an INS functionary was on the witness stand testifying in the courtroom of United States District Court Judge Earl Carroll. The witness explained that the INS had sent Cruz and Graham out to spy on worship services in Tucson, Phoenix and Nogales and that they had even recorded the entire October 1, 1984 ecumenical service at Camelback Presbyterian Church in Phoenix. As if that were not enough, the INS official went on to testify that the government was prepared to "do it again."

Although Judge Carroll refused to dismiss the indictments, he was dis-turbed enough by the spying to say, on the record, that "the whole process has been sullied, in a sense, by the informers and their recorders." Stung by the judge's criticism, the prosecutor assured Judge Carroll that the tape "at the [Camelback] Presbyterian church on this occasion" was not "part of the government's case" and that the government "will not use" that tape in presenting its criminal case to a jury. From that point, the government's criminal case against the Sanctuary Movement workers disintegrated into a fractious eight-month trial that ended in a welter of three acquittals, eight convictions, and two successive appeals.

Meanwhile, the government's tape recording of the October 1, 1984 ecumenical service took on a life of its own. A gusher of national publicity followed the courtroom revelation on May 23, as wire services, newspapers, cartoons, editorials, television, magazines, and radio all focused on the story about "spies in churches." For years, there had been dark suspicions about government snoops in churches, especially during the Vietnam War; and the California Department of Corrections had once placed a radio transmitter in the chapel of a juvenile detention facility for "security purposes." However, the INS recording of the October 1 service was, evidently, the first documented proof that the United States Government had actually spied on open, lawful, mainstream American religious services.

The reactions were mixed. Officially, the Tucson and Phoenix Catholic Dioceses ignored the spying in their Masses, though many of their clergy were up in arms. The three Presbyterian churches and one Lutheran church that had been infiltrated were not so passive. Quickly, these small, Protestant congregations examined the effects from the government spies in their services and decided to "do something," without knowing what.

At Alzona Lutheran Church — a mission church in the Phoenix barrio — the Sunday evening Spanish language Bible Study Group ended altogether because Hispanics were afraid to attend. At the upscale Camelback Presbyterian Church and Sunrise Presbyterian Church, some "law and order" members quit, believing that their churches had acted "illegally" and had gotten exactly what they deserved from the government. At Southside Presbyterian Church, which is located in an economically depressed area of Tucson, members discovered that the INS had even planted a woman who posed as a "volunteer" and who actually worked in the church office.

At each of these affected Protestant churches, strangers were regarded with suspicion, sermons were delivered on the assumption they were being taped, attendance fell off, congregants were guarded in their audible prayers, and pastoral counseling and church meetings were often avoided out of concerns about privacy. When the Internal Revenue Service audited church members, some people believed it was connected with the spying. When one

Lutheran activist lost his security clearance, he assumed the worst.

Within weeks, the national Presbyterian and Lutheran denominations became involved. On July 16, 1985, Bishop David W. Preus and other officials from the American Lutheran Church (which later became the Evangelical Lutheran Church in America) met in Washington, D.C., with Alan Nelson, who was the INS Commissioner and who was also a Lutheran. When Bishop Preus asked Commissioner Nelson for assurances that there would be no more government spies in worship services, the Commissioner politely but firmly refused to give any such assurances and said that the INS had to keep that option open.

Later, Lutheran officials joined Rev. James E. Andrews, the Stated Clerk and head of The Presbyterian Church (U.S.A.), in a call for a Congressional investigation. Representative Don Edwards, who chairs a House subcommittee on civil rights, was interested in holding hearings but they never happened.

At first, nobody suggested a lawsuit and for good reason: the issue of spies in churches had never before been faced by the federal courts. Neither the First Amendment — which explicitly protects the "free exercise of religion" — nor the Fourth Amendment — which prohibits "unreasonable searches and seizures" — had ever been applied to curb governmental spying on religious services.

In the past, surveillance programs had been challenged not by religious worshipers but rather by political activists, civil rights crusaders and anti-war protestors whom the government was keeping tabs on. In rejecting virtually every one of these lawsuits, the courts analyzed the First Amendment and the Fourth Amendment in such a narrow way that the sacred values inherent in worship — faith, trust, and openness — were left defenseless to the infiltration of government spies and tape recordings.

For example, in 1972, the United States Supreme Court confronted a case filed by citizens who had been secretly monitored by the U.S. Army for their anti-war activities and who asserted claims under the First Amendment.

To maintain such a case, the Supreme Court said, the plaintiffs must have suffered tangible, objective and non-speculative damage from the surveillance, such as the loss of money or property. Since the plaintiffs complained about fear and anxiety and since these problems were deemed "abstract," "subjective" and "conjectural" by the Court, the case was lost. For religion and for worship in particular, the consequences from the Supreme Court's analysis were profound.

The core of religion is not property or money or anything "objective" or "tangible." Faith is "abstract." Love is "subjective." Trust is "conjectural." Indeed, two of the great commandments are based upon so-called abstractions: "Thou shalt love the Lord thy God with all thy heart and all thy soul and with all thy mind" and "Thou shalt love thy neighbor as thyself." Were these "abstract" values beyond the scope of the First Amendment? Would the courts require a physical, objective or non-speculative loss before these "abstract" and "subjective" values could be protected? Nobody knew the answers because the courts had never faced the issues.

Similar uncertainties existed in the Fourth Amendment context in which police must have warrants or some probable cause to believe there is evidence of illegality before they can search a house or tape record a private conversation. By inviting saints and sinners alike into worship, do churches intend their services to be "public" rather than "private?" By praying together out loud, do congregants "consent" to the government's clandestine monitoring or taping of their spiritual communications? Again, there were no legal answers.

I am a lawyer in a large Phoenix law firm and, without ever knowing why, I offered, in the Summer of 1985, to sue the federal government for the churches and their denominations. Maybe I did it because my wife and daughter had attended the taped, October 1, 1984 ecumenical service. Maybe it was out of profound admiration for Rev. John Fife, who, tough as a hardwood pew, had helped found the Sanctuary Movement and was later convicted in the criminal case.

Whatever my motives, I assembled a team of lawyers, including my wife Sara (who had successfully litigated her own First Amendment case before the United States Supreme Court in 1971), and my partner, Janet Napolitano (who later would represent Professor Anita Hill in the controversial Clarence Thomas Supreme Court confirmation hearings and who still later would become Governor of the State of Arizona). My wary law partners agreed that the firm would support this case without compensation but hoped, for financial reasons, that we would either win or lose as fast and as cheaply as possible.

In our planning sessions, the church representatives adamantly opposed any claim for money for damages or even for lawyers' fees. What they wanted was a binding judicial precedent that would limit governmental spying on worship services to situations in which the government had a warrant or had a compelling reason to believe that foul play would occur or critical evidence would be lost.

After hundreds of hours of research, we drafted what is called a complaint, which, when filed with the court, would initiate this case against the federal government. On the first page, we listed the plaintiffs — the four Protestant congregations and their two parent denominations — and then, after the "versus" or "v." symbol, named each defendant — Jesus Cruz, Solomon Graham, the federal government and several INS bureaucrats. Just before the complaint went into final form, I noticed to my horror that the lead plaintiff was *Presbyterian Church (U.S.A.)* and the that lead defendant was "Jesus Cruz," meaning that the short-form name for this case would have become *Presbyterian Church v. Jesus.* That would never do; so we changed the sequence of defendants and the case became known as *Presbyterian Church v. United States of America* or, for us, "the church case."

On January 13, 1986, we filed this case of first impression in the Arizona federal district court and generated news on virtually every radio station, TV station, and newspaper in the country. The next day, on January 14, 1986, *The New York Times* ran a front-page story, "Churches Sue U.S., Alleging

Illegal Acts In Inquiry on Aliens." *The Los Angeles Times,* on page two, carried the story and photograph of determined clergymen under the caption: "2 Churches Sue U.S. Over INS Infiltration." Initially, we liked the publicity, hoping it would arouse popular support and generate pressure on the government.

By remarkable good luck, Charles L. Hardy was assigned to this case and he was the one judge we wanted more than anybody else. Judge Hardy is a deeply religious, liberal Democrat who had been appointed to the bench by President Carter after a distinguished career as a state court trial judge. If there was anyone on the bench in Arizona who would appreciate the importance of protecting the "free exercise of religion" then it surely was Judge Hardy, we reasoned. We all felt a surge of optimism.

Within days, the churches' good fortune got even better. Late in January 1986, the United States State Department released a Bulletin entitled, "Religion in Eastern Europe," and denounced the Soviet "spy system" in its churches. As the State Department put it, Soviet spies in churches deprived citizens "of their religious freedom." If that was true in the Soviet Union, then surely the same should be true in the United States. We planned to play the State Department off against the Justice Department.

Soon after the case was filed, a team of Justice Department lawyers in Washington, D.C. appeared for the government and immediately implemented a hard-nosed defense strategy. Specifically, the Justice Department lawyers withheld any documents concerning Operation Sojourner; they refused to make Cruz and Graham available for a formal, on-the-record interview called a deposition; and, on May 29, 1986, they filed a written motion to dismiss the churches' case altogether, asking Judge Hardy to throw the case out without holding a trial or deciding the merits.

According to the government's motion, the churches had not lost any "objective" or "tangible" property from the spying, had suffered only "subjective" and "speculative" losses, and therefore could not maintain this lawsuit under the First Amendment. The government also said that the churches worship services were open to the public; that worshipers did not expect any real privacy in their prayers and liturgy; and, consequently, that Cruz and Graham could monitor and tape record services without a warrant or probable cause to believe that any foul play was going to occur.

Significantly, the government did not deny the unappetizing facts about body-bugs, Cruz, Graham, Operation Sojourner, tape recording, the October 1, 1984 ecumenical service or the adverse impact on the congregations' prayers, trust, attendance, counseling and services. Armed with these facts, the churches conceded that their damages were largely "abstract," "subjective," and "conjectural" but met the government head-on by saying that the First Amendment protected the "free exercise" of religion, not just "objective" or "tangible" church property or "physical assets." The churches also conceded that their services were "open" to the "public" but countered by explaining how the public was invited in for the sacred and limited purpose of worship and not for any other activity, such as monitoring, tape recording or, as a ridiculous example, practicing the trombone.

In presenting their case, the churches went beyond the legalities and demonstrated how government spies historically had threatened the fragile sanctity of worship where people are open, vulnerable and trusting. In *Galatians* 2:4, the Apostle Paul warned of false brethren who spy and destroy the fellowship of Christ. Luke 20:20 recounts perhaps the most famous spy story of all, as informants delivered up Jesus' "words" to the government. By the Twentieth Century, none of this had changed and, to prove that point, we quoted the State Department's denunciation of Soviet spies in worship services.

Beyond the legal and the historical, the churches solicited "amici" — or friends of the court — and asked for written support from other denominations. Despite the infiltration of its own Masses and the involvement by its own clergy in the Sanctuary Movement, the Roman Catholic Dioceses were not ready to commit but did so later. For reasons of approval or indifference, the Mormons also said no, permanently. However, signing on were the American Jewish Committee, The National Council of Churches, the American Baptist Churches in the U.S.A., the Baptist Joint Committee on Public Affairs, the Disciples of Christ, the Unitarian Universalist Association, the United Church of Christ, the Jewish Federation of Greater Phoenix, the Southwest Conference of the United Methodist Church, and the Society of Friends.

Convinced by our own arguments, impressed by the support from other denominations, and buoyed up by Judge Hardy's assignment to this case, we did what lawyers should never do, especially in a ground-breaking case like this one: assume that Judge Hardy would deny the government's motion to dismiss.

On October 14, 1986, Judge Hardy held a hearing on the government's motion to dismiss the "church case." There was no jury; there were no witnesses; there was simply a courtroom filled with lawyers, clergymen, congregants, INS officials, and the media.

The Justice Department lawyers, who had come out from Washington, conceded the snooping, the taping, the consequences and the lawfulness of the services. However, playing their favorite themes, they stressed the technical reasons why the case should be thrown out and we heard again and again that the churches had sustained no "objective" or "tangible" property loss; that only "subjective," "speculative," and "conjectural" were involved; that the services were "public," not private; and that worshipers had, in effect, "consented" to the spying and taping. With too much righteousness, I excoriated the government for its sacrilegious espionage in a tirade that lasted for over 45 minutes.

When all the lawyers finally shut up and sat down, Judge Hardy paused for a long moment, looked out from his elevated bench and then said, "Well, frankly, it offends me that the government goes snooping into people's churches, but, nonetheless, I am going to grant the motion in favor of the government defendants." Buying the government's position lock, stock and body-bug, Judge Hardy ruled, under the First Amendment, that the "churches have no standing to raise the freedom of religion claim" because they had not lost any property. Since the services were open to the public, Judge Hardy reasoned that "there was no legitimate expectation of privacy" under the Fourth Amendment and the government was free to enter, tape, spy and record. To our amazement, he even went on to say that "churches don't go to heaven, people do," as if that were either provable or relevant.

We were stunned.

The television cameras, microphones and reporters were waiting at the base of the courthouse steps in a feral pack. Shocked and wounded, I approached them and immediately caught a series of hard-edged questions: "What went wrong, Mr. Baird?" "Why did you file a case that was so weak?" "Whose idea was this case, anyway?" "What will you do now?" "How will you explain this to the millions of Lutherans and Presbyterians across the country?" And, within minutes, our defeat was on radio and television and would soon appear the next day in newspapers throughout the country. Suddenly, I did not like publicity.

During the next several days, the news got even worse. For example, there was a follow-up piece in a local Phoenix newspaper that quoted one of our clients, a Lutheran minister, who said: "I don't think our own lawyer was very good because the judge asked questions about the church and he had no answer. He kept arguing the law when he should have been educating the judge as to the nature of the church." Unfortunately, the quote turned out to be accurate.

Even Judge Hardy spoke to the press. In a front-page story in the Sunday, October 19, 1986 edition of the *The Arizona Republic*, Judge Hardy said that the government had been "heavy-handed," that its spying was "not morally justifiable" but that he was compelled, by the controlling law, to throw our case out of court. Some church people read his remarks and wondered out loud how "their lawyers" could have been so blind to the "controlling law."

Apparently, I had brought a nationally publicized defeat down on two major Protestant denominations, four small Arizona churches and my own law firm. To make matters worse, I managed to cost my partners several hundred thousand dollars in legal services for which there was no victory, money, or even the moral credit from a close case. I would have traded Job, straight across.

The intermediate appellate court between the Supreme Court in Washington and Judge Hardy in Phoenix is the Ninth Circuit Court of Appeals, which had its courthouse in the seedy Mission District of San Francisco, right across the street from the bus station. The Ninth Circuit scheduled the hearing on the churches' appeal for 10:00 a.m. on July 14, 1987.

Before leaving for the Ninth Circuit courthouse from our downtown San Francisco hotel, I did something out of character: Early in the morning, I hiked up to the top of Nob Hill, made my way to The Grace Cathedral and sat there for some 30 minutes in Gothic splendor, wondering what in the hell I was doing and why. There was no phony prayer, blinding epiphany, or battlefield conversion. Instead, what came was an overdue appreciation of the stakes: the ability of people of faith to join together, in stained-glass elegance or gray-walled squalor, and to open up to God and each other, without the slightest concern about government spies or recording devices. Even in collective worship, prayer is still one-on-one and it is conducted on a private line with God, not a party line connected to the Justice Department or the INS.

Energized, I walked out of The Grace Cathedral, silently repeating the passage from *Romans* 12:19: "vengeance is mine sayeth the Lord." If the Lord needed any help later in the morning, I was ready.

In an appellate court such as the Ninth Circuit, there are no juries or witnesses, only a panel of judges — usually three — who sit in robes behind their elevated bench and throw questions at lawyers who present oral argument from a lectern. Each side is given 20 minutes to persuade these judges, who have already read extensive written briefs, either to reverse or affirm the decision of the trial court.

The gavel sounded. "All rise" said the bailiff. And a full gallery came to its feet, as three robed judges filed in and took their seats. Judge Anderson was a polite, conservative Republican from Idaho; Judge Norris was a truculent, liberal Democrat from Southern California; and Judge Leavy, who had recently been appointed by President Reagan, had the reputation of being a fair-minded moderate from Oregon.

Representing the churches, I went to the lectern first and immediately attacked the myth of "criminality" that the government had written about in its briefs. According to the government, the churches were attempting to "create a safe haven for criminal conduct" and this "criminality" tainted the October 1 ecumenical service and justified the spying and taping. This was an easy charge to refute because all the judges had to do was listen to the October 1, 1984 tape and then read what the Justice Department lawyers had told Judge Hardy: "nothing remotely illegal occurred at those services."

The appellate judges understood that there was nothing criminal about the services. However, they wanted to know if governmental curiosity or the mere "possibility of wrongdoing" could have justified the snooping. Having anticipated this question, I answered it this way: Surely because a church chooses to embrace a controversial topic — whether it be abortion or disarmament or refugee rights or prison conditions or drug use or whatever — to pray, to have sermons on about these subjects, to educate, to learn and to reach for their Maker for understanding, does not give the government an open door to conclude that they have a sound basis for criminal activity that warrants their investigations. More than anything else, the judges wanted to know whether the churches had sustained the kind of "tangible" or "objective" damage that, in traditional legal terms, would be required as a precondition to a First Amendment challenge to governmental surveillance. My response was as follows: We wish to meet the government head-on when they say that there are subjective values at stake here and that those values are unprotected by the constitution. We submit that the very core of religion is subjective. It is trust, it is faith, it is openness, and those virtues are protected by the First Amendment. Religion, as protected by the First Amendment, is not buildings, pews, and collection plates but rather, at its heart, is the very set of speculative and subjective values that the government downplayed in the trial court and destroyed by its spying. Suddenly, my 20 minutes were up and I sat down, adrenaline flowing. As the judges started pounding the Justice Department lawyer with some wonderfully difficult questions, I went from a state of competitive exhilaration to something the Germans call *schadenfreude* — "feeling pleasure at someone else's misfortune."

In response to the Judge Norris' questions, the government lawyer admitted that the services were legal, that the congregations had not consented to sharing their prayers with the INS, and that the churches had indeed been adversely affected by a loss of trust, openness, and attendance. The most revealing moment came when the government's lawyer was forced to admit that, as far as the government was concerned, its "agents and informants can go sit in any church anywhere." Incredulous, Judge Norris asked, "Does that mean that the government has a license, under the First Amendment, to infiltrate and to hinder the free exercise of religion in all of the hundreds of churches in Arizona?" The government attorney responded, "Yes, Your Honor."

All three judges were stunned. My *schadenfreude* became radioactive.

On March 15, 1989 — almost two years after the oral argument — the Ninth Circuit Court of Appeals unanimously reversed Judge Hardy's decision in a 22-page opinion. As if written in heaven, the Ninth Circuit Judges rejected almost every reason advanced by Judge Hardy for dismissing the churches' lawsuit.

On the key issue of First Amendment, the Ninth Circuit said that the churches had indeed suffered the kind of damage that would permit this First Amendment challenge to the surveillance. Rejecting the government's contention that the churches needed to sustain some kind of objective, physical, or tangible loss, the court said that the churches' "injuries are not speculative; they are palpable and direct." The court elaborated as follows: "As a result of the surveillance of worship services, members have withdrawn from active participation in the churches, a bible study group has been canceled for lack of participation, clergy time has been diverted from regular pastoral duties, support for the churches has declined, and congregants have become reluctant to seek pastoral counseling and are less open in prayers and confessions." For the first time in our country's history, a federal court had recognized that the First Amendment's "free exercise" clause reached beyond the "objective" and the "tangible" and protected the sacred, subjective core of all worship: openness, trust, and faith. Immediately, the churches' victory hit the wire services, newspapers, and electronic media. National publicity was good again.

After the Ninth Circuit opinion was rendered, the case was sent back to Phoenix to a different trial judge — Roger G. Strand, a quiet, patient jurist who was appointed by President Reagan and who has, as his best quality, the ability to separate his personal views from his official rulings. The Ninth Circuit had instructed him to decide whether the spying was still going on and, if it was, to enter a ruling that would be consistent with its opinion. During the summer of 1989, we formulated a simple strategy: publicly interview Jesus Cruz and Solomon Graham; expose their criminality; and show just how sleazy Operation Sojourner really had been. In the process, we expected to establish that the government was still spying on worship services because there were reports from all over the country of mysterious break-ins of churches which had aided Central Americans.

Faced with our demands to interview Cruz and Graham and to expose the underside of Operation Sojourner, the government cut a deal with us: if the churches would hold off interviewing Cruz and Graham, then the Justice Department would agree that the covert surveillance was still going on or could resume at any minute. Evidently, the Justice Department believed that, by this deal, it would keep Cruz and Graham under wraps and give its lawyers time to file another round of technical motions.

After signing the stipulation, the churches did not give the government a chance to file anything. Instead, the churches immediately asked the trial judge to rule for the churches without ever holding a trial. Since the government had conceded all the facts and had even stipulated that the spying was still going on or could resume at any time, the churches pressed Judge Strand for a ruling on the legality of spies in worship services.

At 10:00 a.m. on February 5, 1990, Judge Strand listened as the lawyers argued over whether government spies could be in churches. At the end of more than two hours, Judge Strand took the case under advisement.

On December 10, 1990, Judge Strand rendered his 23-page opinion. If government agents had probable cause to believe that a crime was being committed or that vital evidence was about to be lost, then Judge Strand said that the government could investigate worship services without a warrant. However, Judge Strand went on to mine some First Amendment gold and write as follows:

> "Plaintiffs, in the free exercise of their constitutionally protected religious activities, are protected against governmental intrusion in the absence of a good faith purpose for the subject investigation. The government is constitutionally precluded from unbridled and inappropriate covert activity which has as it purpose or objective the abridgment of the first amendment freedoms of those involved. Additionally, the participants involved in such investigation must adhere scrupulously to the scope and extent of the invitation to participate that may have been extended or offered to them." That last sentence had major implications: unless they had a warrant or probable cause, then government agents must *"adhere scrupulously to the scope and extent of the invitation to participate that may have been extended or offered to them."*

This meant that, if undercover agents had nothing more than curiosity, then they could not violate the invitation to worship, they had to adhere "scrupulously to the scope and extent of the invitation" and they could not enter those services for the inconsistent purposes of taping or spying. Finally, after more than five years of work, patience, disappointment and uncertainty, four little Arizona churches and their two denominations gave the national media the best story of all: for the first time in our nation's history, there were judicially imposed limits on government spying on worship services. *The New York Times,* in its December 12, 1990 edition, carried a six-column story about Judge Strand's decision under the headline, "U.S. Judge Limits Government Spies at Church." Unhappy about losing, the government asked Judge Strand to change his mind. Judge Strand held fast to his opinion but extended the government's appeal deadline into the summer of 1991. On August 23, 1991, the Associated Press ran a national wire service story and announced the government's decision not to appeal Judge Strand's ruling. In the absence of an appeal, Judge Strand's opinion was published in the law books, became a binding precedent and limited the government's surveillance capabilities from that point forward.

A few months later, there was a post-script. During the weeks leading up to December 15, 1991 when America celebrated the bicentennial of the Bill of Rights, a series of public service radio spots ran throughout the country in which former, living Presidents commented on the importance of the first ten amendments to our Constitution. Either forgetting or perhaps never even knowing about his own Administration's policy of sending spies and body-bugs into worship services, Ronald Reagan used his air time to explain how the First Amendment protected "the free exercise of religion." "Because of the First Amendment," President Reagan said, "we in this country do not have to worry about government spies in churches."

Amen, Mr. President.

Post 9-11 Freedom and Security

Shortly after Japan bombed Pearl Harbor on December 7, 1941, the U.S. Army built two camps in western Arizona that, though long gone, have lessons to teach us about post-September 11 freedom and security. Both camps had barracks, barbed wire and armed guards but their differences are what make them relevant today.

One installation was Camp Horn near Yuma where my father and the Army's 81St Division trained before getting shipped off to the South Pacific for battle. The soldiers there had lost their civilian freedoms by enlistment, which is a free choice, or by conscription, which is sanctioned by the Constitution.

The other installation was Camp Poston near the farming village of Poston, just east of the Colorado River. Although officially called "Relocation Centers," Camp Poston and other camps like it were in fact prison camps where over 120,000 men, women and children were incarcerated solely because of their Japanese ancestry. Although officially created in response to national security concerns, Camp Poston and other camps like it were in fact created in response to fear, hysteria and racism.

On February 19, 1942, President Franklin Roosevelt signed Executive Order 9066 and, over the objections of Attorney General Francis Biddle and FBI Director J. Edgar Hoover, authorized military commanders to exclude anyone from designated areas to prevent "sabotage and espionage." In March, 1942, Army General John DeWitt issued Public Proclamations that excluded persons of Japanese ancestry from the entire Pacific Coast and Congress promptly made it a crime to violate those Proclamations. Thus, 77,000 American citizens and 43,000 resident aliens were rounded up, branded as traitors and incarcerated without charges, evidence or trial.

Shamefully, the courts let it happen.

In an Opinion that will, like the attack on Pearl Harbor, live in infamy, the United States Supreme Court, on December 18, 1944 and by a six-to-three vote, held that these detentions were constitutional. In *Koramatsu v. The United States,* the Supreme Court called the confinements "temporary exclusions," pretended that "Mr. Koramatsu was not excluded from the Military Areas because of hostility to him or his race," and said that courts should defer to the government in wartime.

Fortunately, September 11, 2001 did not ignite the same degree of fear, hysteria, and racism as did December 7, 1941. Nevertheless, September 11 did generate mass arrests, secret confinements, and indefinite detentions of Arabs living in America; it prompted the hasty passage of the USA Patriot Act; and it triggered new, open-ended Justice Department rules on surveillance and immigration. In resolving the conflicts between freedom and security that these post-September 11 measures have produced, Camps Horn and Poston are instructive.

One lesson is that, no matter how outrageous the provocation, security measures that restrict domestic freedom must be tested by the logic of necessity. Camp Horn was obviously necessary and Camp Poston was obviously not. Indeed, the irony is that Camp Poston weakened national security because, at a time when there was a manpower shortage and America needed Japanese speakers, Camp Poston confined thousands of able-bodied citizens who could have helped the war effort.

When the post-September 11 security measures are tested by the logic of necessity, some are justified while others are not. For example, additional airport security is warranted, including searches, x-rays, metal detectors, and profiling for the likes of Timothy McVeigh and Osama Bin Laden. Furthermore, given the cellular mobility of today's population, the USA Patriot Act sensibly authorizes warrants for nationwide wiretaps, regardless of specific location or telephone number.

However, necessity has yet to be shown for the unrestricted surveillance provisions in the USA Patriot Act and the new Justice Department Rules. For example, why should the F.B.I. be permitted, without probable cause, to monitor churches, synagogues, mosques, political meetings and internet chat rooms? Why should the USA Patriot Act permit the secret arrest and detention of immigrants who are not suspected of terrorism and whose only transgressions, if they exist at all, are technical visa violations? Why should these prisoners be indefinitely held incommunicado without charges, counsel, bond or hearing? Is it wise, at a time when America needs Arab friends and Arabic speakers, to alienate the Arab-American community with mass arrests and secret detentions?

Another important lesson from Camps Horn and Poston is that domestic security measures must always be tested by the rule of law. During World War Two, everything was lawful about Camp Horn and nothing was lawful about Camp Poston. To make matters worse, America's courts supported these illegal detentions and the victims had to wait 40 years for justice.

Eventually, in 1988, Congress passed and President Reagan signed the Civil Liberties Restoration Act of 1988 which appropriated millions of dollars for reparations to survivors of Relocation Centers like Camp Poston. According to Congress, these reparations were intended to redress wrongs of the past and to "discourage the occurrence of similar injustices and violations of civil liberties in the future." Indeed, Congress made this extraordinary apology on behalf of the Nation:

> "The Congress recognizes that a grave injustice was done to both citizens and permanent resident aliens of Japanese ancestry by the evacuation, relocation and internment of civilians during World War Two ... The actions were carried out without adequate security reasons and without any acts of sabotage ... and were motivated largely by racial prejudice, wartime hysteria and a failure of political leadership ... For these fundamental violations of basic civil liberties and constitutional rights of these individuals of Japanese ancestry, the Congress apologizes on behalf of the Nation."

Perhaps times have changed because, in the wake of the post-September 11 security measures, courts have not been blindly deferential and they have ruled against the government on such issues as secret arrests, closed deportation hearings, access to counsel and non-disclosure of names. However, the Supreme Court has yet to be heard from and Chief Justice Rhenquist has said, reminiscent of the *Koramatsu* decision, that in time of war the law "speaks with a muted voice." At Camp Poston, the law spoke "with a muted voice." The silence was deafening.

CHAPTER SIX

LAWYER

MIND, MAGIC, MISTAKES AND MANNERS

A Lawyer Battles Depression

Magician In The Courtroom

My Stupid Mistakes

Deskside Manners

A Lawyer Battles Depression

My distempers first went public in front of 123 lawyers. Even though I was not scheduled to speak at the law firm retreat, I suddenly commandeered the microphone and started denouncing my partners and associates for their "incompetence" and "malpractice." After 15 minutes of this invective, our managing partner ended the clamor by adjourning the meeting and opening the bar. Undaunted, I continued, in between belts of straight scotch, to blast lawyers I cared for and I even brought one to tears.

On the Monday following the retreat, an angry deputation of senior partners paid me a surprise visit. The meeting lasted only five minutes and it took place in my twenty-third floor corner office which, years earlier, I had plastered with diplomas from fancy schools, framed newspaper articles about high-profile legal victories, photographs of my family and a certificate of membership in an academic fraternity.

My visitors were hostile and blunt. According to them, I had been "destructive," "cruel," and "wrong" at the retreat. Even worse, I was "tearing the firm apart" by demanding "too much from everybody." Their parting exhortations were "see somebody" and "get help!"

See somebody? Get help? Who did they think they were talking to? Some hallucinating nut who thought unseen enemies were tapping phone calls and hiding under my bed? A helpless, thumb-sucker who couldn't tie his own shoes? I wasn't like that at all. Instead, I was a hard-driving, rainmaking young partner who had already won a case at the United States Supreme Court and who had brought mega-bucks into the firm. What had set me off at the retreat was that other partners and associates weren't pulling their loads, putting in the hours or winning the cases that I was. Shouldn't the firm care about that? I was pissed!

Over the course of the next week, my fury gradually subsided and I spent several hours each night walking rather than sleeping or working. Eventually, from somewhere below my neck — in a region where life juices slosh and ferment and sometimes seep out as truth — it came to me that my senior partners were probably right. Upon further walking and reflecting, I realized that they didn't even know the half of it.

Despite the happy family photographs on my office walls, I was constantly haranguing my children for simply being children and my marriage was becoming cold, distant, and silent. Despite the framed newspaper articles, diplomas and certificate from that learned fraternity, I secretly felt over my head, inadequate, not smart enough; I constantly needed approval, even adulation; and I was sure that my achievements were overachievements, resulting not from talent but rather from punishing, around-the-clock work habits that I couldn't maintain much longer. In addition to the outbursts at my colleagues, there were screaming, walking, talking nightmares that once put me in the hospital with a severed toe.

The worst part, however, was an inky darkness that colored my outlook with a bleak negativity and also made me feel as though I was always just one mistake away from my doom and undoing. Sometimes, I couldn't define what that doom was or how I would be undone, only that it scared the hell out of me and I knew I couldn't survive it. At other times, I could define those fears and they ranged from failing as a father, losing my marriage, or being exposed as a hack lawyer.

Since I didn't have a "somebody" to "see," I placed a series of confidential telephone calls and compiled a list of names from friends and physicians. Feeling ashamed about needing "help" for myself, I lied and said that I was looking "on behalf of a client." "My client doesn't need a high-powered psychiatrist," I explained, "just somebody low-key to help sort out a few, everyday problems." Right.

The first "somebody" I saw was a kind, soft-spoken woman psychologist who announced, at the end of our first session, that I was "seriously depressed."

Seriously depressed? That couldn't be because, as I authoritatively informed her, "depressed people weren't hard-chargers like me, they were down-in-the-dumps types who spent their days in bed, curled up in fetal positions." All she said, and very nicely, was, "You're wrong."

In her view, my deceased mother was "the key" to my depression. "You and your mother were very close," the psychologist observed correctly. "You were an only child; your father was a violent alcoholic; she died when you were a teenager; and you never grieved for her." The psychologist also explained that she would use a method called "transactional analysis" and so, for months, she drew diagrams — consisting of lines, arrows, X's and O's — that vaguely resembled football plays book. The diagrams didn't help and, eventually, I quit and decided to take care of myself.

From racks alongside grocery store checkout lines, in health food stores and at book sellers, I bought a stack of paperback books with titles like, *"Chase The Blues Away With Vitamins;" "Exercising Your Body And Elevating Your Mood;"* and *"Relaxation: The Path To Mental Health."* But the megavitamins were huge, brown chokers that I often gagged on and that didn't even produce a placebo effect. Running every day inflicted painful shin-splints but didn't generate any of the exhilarating endorphins that skinny people like to talk about at cocktail parties. And the relaxation exercises were worthless because, straining as hard as possible, I couldn't concentrate on my heartbeat or breathing for more than twenty seconds before I started worrying about a pressing problem or something that I had forgotten to do.

When the self-help didn't help, I went back to my list of "somebodies who were good," selected a name and saw a board-certified psychiatrist. He was fun to talk to; he loved NBA basketball; he wasn't interested in diagrams, lines, arrows, X's, O's; and he thought my failed, vitamin-exercise-relaxation program was pretty. funny. According to him, I was depressed, all right, but my depression came from a radioactive perfectionism in which losing a lawsuit could scald my soul; a car rattle could take my eyes off the road and hands off the wheel; and a drippy faucet could keep me up all night with wrenches, buckets and rags. After spending over a year comparing the Suns with the Lakers and trying to loosen me up with suggestions about emotional detachment, this easy-going doctor suddenly died in a Caribbean skin-diving accident and left me to mourn for myself and consult the psychiatrist who purchased his practice.

The new doctor turned out to be a Yale-trained, Freudian "analyst." He wanted me flat on my back and he thought that the source of my problems was the 15-year estrangement from my oversized, combat-veteran, physician father who, when I was a kid, demanded total obedience and superperformance. After nine months of my droning on about my father's boozy violence and after hearing only an occasional "I see" or "uh huh" from the psychiatrist, I was jolted when he predicted that my treatment would take six more years of weekly sessions at $135 an hour. That was too long and too expensive. Abruptly, I ended our weekly talk show.

Frustrated and feeling worse, I saw my internist. He thought that medication was the answer and, consequently, sent me to a pharmaco-logically-minded psychiatrist. At the end of a perfunctory, get-acquainted interview, the new psychiatrist handed me a prescription for a drug called Pertofrane; he said he was leaving on a short vacation; and he suggested that I "check in" with him in "a few weeks."

Pertofrane didn't elevate my mood at all. Instead, it dried my mouth, scrambled my mind, and, of all things, ballooned my prostate up into the size of an excruciating tennis ball. Unable to reach my new, vacationing psychiatrist, I throbbed for an entire weekend with an enlarged gland that, before this time, I barely even knew I had.

Dry, dizzy and swollen, I went back to my internist on the following Monday. He took me off Pertofrane; he let my prostate deflate; and then he prescribed lithium. As I learned later, lithium was a natural salt that is found in the alkaline waters the Romans liked to bathe in; the Victorians mistakenly thought it cured gout; and, in 1949, an Australian doctor found that it moderated the bi-polar symptoms of manic depression.

Even though I lacked any manic symptoms, lithium improved my mood; brightened my outlook; and did so without enlarging a single gland. After a few weeks, I was humming tunes, cracking jokes, forgetting torments, accepting the present, and facing the future with fewer apprehensions. Lithium made my hands tremble, increased my weight, affected my short term memory, and required frequent urination. However, these side-effects were tolerable triflings and well worth my better disposition.

Over the course of two years, however, my mood deteriorated; my hands quaked; I gained 25 pounds; my memory was terrible; and, worst of all, that inky darkness came flooding back. Indeed, after a grueling four-and-half-week jury trial, lithium failed me altogether and, once again, life seemed unbearable and suicide seemed sensible. Desperate, I drove down to the University of Arizona College of Medicine in Tucson.

"You have an interesting form of depression," the Chief of Psychiatry said after taking a thorough history. "You may be one of the most driven yet depressed patients I've ever treated." He went on: "Most people with this powerful a form of depression are either marginally functional or end up in the hospital." "You, on the other hand," he continued, "react to depression with control and energy that have yielded success but have caused you great pain and exhaustion." I agreed.

"I want you on a new drug called Prozac," he directed. "In addition, we'll get you into regular therapy in Phoenix with someone with whom you have the right fit and with whom you can find practical solutions to the problems of lawyering, parenting, husbanding and just plain living."

I balked. Years of therapy, even with board-certified psychiatrists, had done little. Besides, I had heard horror stories about Prozac and had read about lawsuits in which plaintiffs blamed this drug for everything from suicide to homicide to nymphomania.

"We'll acclimate you to Prozac in micro-doses," the medical school psychiatrist explained. "Pour cranberry juice into an eight-ounce measuring cup; empty one 20 milligram capsule of Prozac into the juice; and start by drinking just two ounces a day." "Don't worry about any side effects," he said, "we'll slowly increase the dosage over time and you shouldn't have any trouble at all."

Without side effects, Prozac blew my dark clouds far enough apart so I could feel some sunshine and see some reality. Even better, the medical school physician referred me to a wise and insightful local psychiatrist who helped me understand what survival patterns I had adopted as a kid in a violent, alcoholic home and how those same behavior patterns had brought me achievement as an adult but destruction as a man, father, and husband. For example, I could, as a kid, avoid my father's wrath if I never expressed my own feelings, if I always adapted to him, and if I was a superstar. But, as an adult, I needed to know what I felt and to express those feelings in order to get and give the emotional essentials of life that were more important than power, money, or success. Besides, perfection was impossible for anyone to achieve and, in the long run or maybe short run, it was going to kill me.

Six years later, I'm still a "recovering" depression victim. I have a joyous, new marriage. I'm in a weekly support group. I'm taking another drug called Zoloft.

Everyday, I practice figuring out my feelings and then work hard at voicing them as my subjective, emotional "truths." No longer do I need approval, adulation, awards, diplomas, or legal victories to think of myself as competent. My doom and undoing are no longer one step away. I can enjoy clouds, birds, rain, sunshine, children, magic, art, music. And there isn't a single diploma on my office walls anymore and the certificate from that learned fraternity is in storage somewhere.

My partners were right. I needed to "see somebody" and to "get help." For all my somebodies and for all their help, I am grateful.

Magician In The Courtroom

Magic first came to me in a small, rural Utah town in the 1940's when one of the most exciting summer events was the irregular appearance of a traveling novelty shop that would park under a large shade tree on Main Street and sell bug-eyed country kids handshake buzzers, itching powder and, best of all, rudimentary magic tricks. From this weathered van with wooden fold-down side panels, worldly vendors introduced me to ingenious secrets that made coins disappear, cards change color, and neighborhood kids chant "do it again" after each clumsy performance.

In a sense, magic ran in my family. At holidays, my father wowed house guests by vanishing a lighted cigarette in a borrowed handkerchief. For kids, my mother did a crude mind reading routine in which the "mind reader" left the room, an object was chosen and the "reader" returned to miraculously identify the chosen object. My own favorite stunt was to use a marked and tapered "stripper deck" and, in a flash, produce and identify a spectator's previously chosen card.

In those days, magic was a young boy's heaven and, on one occasion, a terrifying hell. When a fundamentalist missionary discovered my stripper deck during a Bible School class, he thunderously denounced the cards as "the devil's bible" and me as "the devil's disciple." Wearing an expression of demonic loathing, he condemned magicians as a vile group and ranted about some unsavory goings-on among the jacks, queens, and kings in the deck. Decades later, I figured out that his horrific reaction probably came from *Revelations* 22:14-15, where idolaters, fornicators, and magicians are biblically and collectively banished from the proverbial city of righteousness. Despite the promise of hell's eternal barbecue, I stayed with magic, accepted my doom, and resigned myself to associating with idolaters and fornicators.

From those early beginnings, magic grew from a boyish hobby into a young man's fascination and, eventually, into a separate, professional career for a practicing lawyer. Yet this evolution proved surprisingly difficult, especially the transition from rank dilettante to working professional. Psychologically, I had to overcome the perception that magic is only for foolish buffoons at little children's birthday parties and not for grown-up lawyers. Then there were the uncountable hours needed to read, take lessons and practice in order to command just a few of the "moves" and "sleights" in this vast field. Finally, the only way to master the elusive techniques of showmanship-like staging, timing, pacing and style-was the hard way of performing again, again, and again.

And so, for years, I gave shows to every type of audience, large and small, drunk and sober, children and adult, reveler and grump. My "stages" were living rooms, clubs, businesses, restaurants, hotels, churches, back-yards, schools, one steamboat on the Mississippi River, and two cruise ships on the Pacific Ocean. Over the course of those appearances, I dropped secret gimmicks, was upstaged by wiseguys, tripped over microphone cords, lost control to kids, got drowned out by drunks, was blinded by spotlights, and committed hundreds of mistakes. Guided by an old saying among magicians that "you have to find places to be bad before you can be good," I found an astounding number of places to be bad and, in the process, discovered part of myself.

Today, my show is called "Illusions of the Mind" and I have presented it to thousands of people at conventions, parties, banquets, conferences and charity balls from San Francisco to Las Vegas, from Palm Springs to Philadelphia, and all over Arizona. Two of the most fun were the 1988 Arizona Judicial Conference in Phoenix and a 1989 Ninth Circuit Judicial Conference in Santa Barbara where I was officially "licensed" to entertain and tease our state and federal judges.

Unlike traditional magic that involves rabbits, hats, ropes and rings, "Illusions of the Mind" is filled with demonstrations of mind reading, mental telepathy and other psychic phenomena. Newspaper headlines are predicted a month in advance. Spectators' friends and pets from over thirty years ago are revealed. The audience even "reads" my mind. Long on humor and short on psychological mumbo jumbo, my show would never please hardcore psychics because I explicitly disclaim any super-duper powers and, instead, fill the evening with spoofs, jokes, and sight gags.

Whether the honoraria were the piddling amounts paid in the old days or $1,000 per show paid today, I have always donated all of the proceeds directly to charity. For the past several years, all fees have gone to the Arizona Cancer Center at the University of Arizona College of Medicine, which is an internationally recognized research and treatment institution and which has received substantial monies from the direct and indirect results of my conjuring.

Yet this avocation has generated more than just fun and philanthropy; surprisingly enough, magic also has produced some unusual insights into the practice of law. While it may be difficult to conceive of lawyers and magicians as being at all alike, there are some remarkable similarities between these two vocations in which practitioners of both professions, with their secrets, privileges and forensic skills, appear before hard-headed skeptics and try to convince them of everything from the ridiculous to the sublime, from the impossible to the obvious. From a lecture I have given to various groups of lawyers called "Law, Magic, and Misdirection," here are, without demonstrative illusions, a few of these off-beat observations that have come from having practiced law and magic simultaneously for more than two decades:

1. Neither lawyers nor magicians traffic in objective reality.
    In a magic show, the audience never sees reality, the lady does not get sawed in half and the tiger does not vanish into thin air. In the law, there is no such thing as absolute reality either because every event, crime, accident, contract, or statute is subject to as many interpretations as there are witnesses to

testify, lawyers to argue and, sadly enough, clients to pay fees.

2. In law and in magic, perception is everything. Magicians want the audience to perceive that the shimmering silver ball is floating freely in mid-air, even though it is doing nothing of the sort. Lawyers want the judge and jury to perceive that their positions are correct, that their opponents are swine and that their own clients are victimized saints, even though these perceptions may be utterly wrong.

3. Magicians and lawyers deliberately manage those perceptions through techniques that are essentially the same: personality, word choice, visual props, histrionics, drama, style, and innuendo. There is no difference between a lawyer's use of a demonstrative exhibit in a courtroom and a magician's use of an enlarged, written display during a show.

4. For lawyers and magicians, form can be as important as content and style is frequently indistinguishable from substance. Without commanding showmanship, mechanically proficient magicians are just dull eccentrics who do strange things. Without a credible presence and an appealing focus, technically skilled lawyers are often dreary robots who lose claims, defenses, guilt, and innocence in a welter of documents, confusion and yawns.

5. Perhaps the most powerful tool for both lawyers and magicians is that of verbal misdirection. Everyone knows that magicians misdirect audiences, that they visually and verbally disguise their dirty work and that they focus attention away from what is really happening. Lawyers also engage in verbal misdirection by "blind-siding" witnesses, focusing attention on strengths and away from weaknesses, substituting jury charm for legal substance, and bobbing and weaving with words to deflect, convince and prevail. With skillful cross examination, lawyers

can make honest witnesses out to be biased, prejudiced, mendacious, or impaired. With creative characterization, lawyers can even change the very character of a set of facts, such as transforming a tort into a contract for statute of limitation purposes.

6. Happily, miracles are not just for magicians, stages, and audiences. Some miracles are for lawyers, courtrooms and clients too. Without magicians, we would never know the wonder of the impossible and the enchantment of a levitation, a "vanish" or a metamorphosis. Without lawyers, separate would today be equal, right to counsel for the poor would not exist, caveat emptor would accompany every sale, most criminal confessions would be extracted in ignorance, and gerrymandered voting districts would be unchecked by constitutional restraint.

There are, of course, vast differences between lawyers and magicians. Lawyers endure hostile opponents, vapid depositions, oppressive interrogatories, confounding delays, judicial rejection, endless paper, painful defeat, and uncomprehending clients. But even in these distinctly legal experiences, there is a place for magic: to transport us beyond the stifling confines of what is and to open up the creative possibilities of what is not. For our clients, our courts, our constitution, and ourselves, may there always be *lex et magus* — law and magic.

My Stupid Mistakes

For the first time in years, I carefully read my bio in Martindale-Hubbell and promptly felt embarrassed, even a little guilty. Although everything in the bio is meticulously accurate about my education, cases, articles, and assorted kudos, the problem is that the cumulative self-glorification may suggest that I am a stranger to stupidity and that I practice law above bone-headedness. Not true.

As the bio reflects, I have spent nearly four decades trying to be seen by judges as ethical, opponents as competent, clients as knowledgeable, and colleagues as dedicated. If fancy ratings, news stories, and unsought awards mean anything, then my efforts have been remarkably successful in generating referrals, fees, flattery and, occasionally, the embarrassment of undeserved recognition.

However, what those ratings, stories and awards don't show and what most judges, opponents, clients, and colleagues don't know is that I have done some really dumb things, especially in the courtroom. First-hand, I have felt the hot flash of self-inflicted humiliation, the sting of warranted rebuke and the self-loathing from unforced errors. More than once have I stood in open court and, with my ears burning and stomach somersaulting, prayed for instant invisibility--to be "beamed up" to anywhere else in the cosmos.

For the sake of colleagues, clients, judges, and friends, it is time that I come clean, confess my bunglings, and set the record straight. For my own sake, it is time to do something I have not done enough of — laugh at myself.

ARIZONA SUPERIOR COURT 1975

It was a bench trial and I represented a paper company and the dispute was over newsprint that had been sold but not paid for. Apart from the salesman's testimony that he sold everything "from wipe to write," the evidence was dull and the judge had every right to be bored. However, in closing argument, I fixed that.

As I rattled on about how the evidence favored the paper company, my brain mindlessly switched from a courtroom speaking mode into an office dictation mode. Suddenly, I started punctuating my argument and said, "Furthermore comma Your Honor comma."

I don't remember how the case turned out, only how I felt when the guffaws erupted.

UNITED STATES SUPREME COURT 1970

The first time I appeared before the United States Supreme Court I was 29 years old. Nervous but cocky, I thought I was on a roll because, just before flying off to Washington, D.C., I had scored a surprise victory in small claims court against a non-lawyer opponent.

Although my client had graduated from Stanford Law School and had been number one on the Arizona Bar Examination, the State Bar would not admit her because she had refused to answer a question on the application that asked whether she had belonged to any organization that advocated the overthrow of the government by force and violence. She had listed all of the organizations that she had ever belonged to and they were, "Girl Scouts, Church Choir, Girls Athletic Association, Young Republicans, Young Democrats, Law Students Civil Rights Research Council, and Stanford Law Association." However, that listing wasn't sufficient for the Bar Examiners.

According to them, she had to answer the question so they could determine what her "political beliefs" were and, if those beliefs were "not acceptable," then they would not admit her. From her perspective, bar applicants could hold any political beliefs they chose because conduct and competence were all that mattered. Moreover, she wanted to take the oath to support the Constitution which, according to an old Supreme Court case, protected political beliefs because they were "inviolate."

Nevertheless, we faced some long odds. Chief Justice Earl Warren had retired; President Nixon had replaced him with Chief Justice Warren Burger; Associate Justice Abe Fortas had resigned under fire; and the United States Supreme Court, in a similar case a few years earlier, had ruled for the California Bar Association. Moreover, the Vietnam War was raging and America was there, the Johnson and Nixon Administrations told us, to fight communism.

Seated next to me at the oral argument was my senior partner who had argued many cases to the Court, who had helped write the briefs and who gave me a "thumbs up" sign when I stood up and took the lectern. After I identified myself but before I could say another word, the questions came at me like hot bullets. "Why do you think a Communist should practice law?" "Wouldn't a Communist lawyer undermine our justice system?" "How can a Communist belief be compatible with the Constitution?"

At first unsettled by the barrage, I stammered that political beliefs were "inviolate" and pointed out that there were hundreds, if not thousands, of lawyers who were racists and, even though those beliefs were incompatible with the Constitution, those lawyers had been admitted to the Bar. My arguments didn't seem to satisfy some of the more aggressive Justices who kept firing questions at me and who, after relentless assaults, succeeded in getting under my skin.

Finally, I had had it with the black-robed aggressors. Out-of-control and out-of-my-mind, I blurted, "if you won't let my client be a lawyer because of her possible beliefs, then you ought to disbar President Nixon because of his actual belief in an unconstitutional war!" There was a stunned silence; my partner buried his face in his hands; and the marble floor trembled beneath my feet.

Two things have stayed with me from that oral argument. First, the satisfaction I felt when President Nixon later resigned in lieu of disbarment. Second, the lesson I learned that every lawyer should know: never piss off the United States Supreme Court.

U S. DISTRICT COURT, NORTHERN DISTRICT OF ILLINOIS 1987

It was a trademark infringement/antitrust case that involved dozens of depositions, multiple motions, two appeals, an order to show cause, and two contempt trials. At one point during the turbulence, I was in court, arguing something to an exhausted and seemingly distracted federal judge when suddenly he was alert, leaning forward and staring down at me with rapt attention. Naturally, I ascribed his interest to my spell-binding oratory, which I put even more energy into until the judge pointed at my chest. I stopped talking, looked down and saw what had attracted his attention.

It was a large, blood-red splotch in my white shirt over the left side of my chest. Before standing up, I had been sitting at counsel table writing with a red felt-tipped pen and, when I stood up to address the court, I had inadvertently put the cap on the wrong end and had pushed the exposed felt tip into my left shirt pocket. Slowly, the red ink soaked into my white shirt and spread until it looked like a bleeding chest wound.

At that moment, I would have preferred a chest wound.

ARIZONA SUPERIOR COURT 2002

Voir dire has never been one of my strengths. When the court permits questions from counsel, I always feel as though I'm flying blind. All too often, I later wish that I had kept my mouth shut.

One such occasion occurred in a legal malpractice case I was defending and, as the *voir dire* process began, I could see several "I-hate-lawyers" expressions on the panelists. The most hateful expression was worn by a lanky, middle-aged man who, in response to a question from the court, angrily announced that he had been through two divorces and, each time, he had despised his lawyers and his wives' lawyers too. Unbidden, he went on to say that, if he were in a boat in the middle of a lake and if a lawyer happened to be out there floundering, he would let that lawyer drown.

When my turn for *voir dire* came, I should have ignored the malcontent and should have been content to strike him. However, being unable to control myself and forgetting that I should say positive things about lawyers, I turned on him and said, "Oh don't worry about a lawyer ever drowning because we can all swim. Didn't you know we're sharks?"

I never asked my client how he liked being called a shark.

ARIZONA SUPERIOR COURT 1999

I have known lawyers who can go to trial without notes, show up with little more than smiles on their faces and vanquish their opponents with memory, charm and guile. These lawyers are few in number and are positively rare in the dull, sprawling tangles of commercial litigation. Anyway, I am not one of those lawyers.

For me, notes are as vital as oxygen for openings, closings and examinations. My notes are detailed with handwritten headings, subjects, deposition pages, exhibit numbers, case citations, and even a few specifically worded questions, explanations, quips, and quotes. As a result, I am a fanatic about making sure that my notes always go with me to court and I always compulsively check my briefcase for them before I leave the office. Never once have I left them behind. However, as I learned to my horror, preparing notes and taking them to trial do not always ensure access to them in the courtroom.

After a difficult, four-week jury trial in a dangerous securities case that our client had refused, re-refused and re-re-refused to settle, the time came for closing argument and, although I was worried about a bad outcome, I was nonetheless prepared for the closing and had my notes with me. Indeed, I knew these notes were in my briefcase because I had, as usual, checked on them before leaving the office.

My briefcase was one of those large, black, heavy-duty affairs with wheels and a combination lock that was frozen in place by a red plastic pin. I never knew the combination because I have a lousy memory for numbers and, besides, I never lock my briefcase. However, on my way to court that day, I must have bumped the briefcase against something because the red plastic pin somehow fell out, allowing the combination dial to rotate.

Imagine the panic of a note-dependent lawyer like myself when my opponent had finished his closing argument and I reached down to open my briefcase and found that it was locked. "Mr. Baird, you may proceed," the judge said, as I frantically twisted the dials first to my birthday, then to my social security number and then my telephone number. No luck.

When the reality sank in that I would never get the combination, I stood up, bent over the briefcase, reached under the lid with both hands and, while visible to everyone in the courtroom, yanked with all my might. Instantly, the lock broke off with a loud "WAAAP," whereupon I grabbed my notes and rushed to the lectern.

As it turned out, "WAAAP" was the only thing the jury remembered about my closing or my case.

U. S. DISTRICT COURT, DISTRICT OF ARIZONA 1986

This blunder is one that I fortunately caught at the last minute but it could have done permanent damage to my client, Presbyterian Church U.S.A., a major Protestant Denomination. The case was a First Amendment free exercise of religion action that Janet Napolitano (now Governor of the State of Arizona) and I filed on behalf of the Presbyterian Church U.S.A. against the federal government and certain undercover agents who had infiltrated and secretly recorded Presbyterian worship services.

What had happened was that, during the civil wars in Central America in the late 1980s, several Presbyterian Churches were taking in Central American refugees who had fled for their lives. However, since the United States supported the military regimes in those countries, the Immigration and Naturalization Service or "INS" had refused, in most instances, to grant these Central Americans "political refugee status" for temporary asylum. Moreover, the Justice Department had also gathered evidence for a criminal prosecution against some of the clergy and congregants by hiring Hispanic undercover agents to pose as worshippers who then, without warrants or probable cause, had secretly recorded prayers, sermons, worship services and confessions of faith.

Our plan was to file a declaratory judgment action against the INS, the Justice Department and the undercover agents and seek a declaration that, before sending spies into worship services, the government had to obtain a warrant or have probable cause to believe there was criminal activity going on. Painstakingly, we drafted a detailed complaint and designated the Presbyterian Church U.S.A. as the lead plaintiff and one of the undercover agents, whose name was Jesus Cruz, as the lead defendant. Just before filing the complaint, I gave the complaint one last read and, to my eye-popping horror, saw that the short caption of the case was going to be "Presbyterian Church U.S.A. v. Jesus."

Deskside Manners

Whenever anyone asks me, "Have you heard the one about the lawyer who...?," I know that a tiresome joke is coming and it will probably involve sharks, leeches or the blistering fires of hell. However, since these jokes are based on stereotypes that come from bad lawyers I can't do anything about, I tolerate the dig, wrench a smile and force a chuckle.

Whenever I come across an opinion poll that ranks professions by their public esteem, I know that lawyers will be down near the bottom, along with car salesmen and undertakers. However, since lawyers inhabit a justice system that invariably generates losers and frequently produces winners who are losers too, I shrug off our unpopularity as just something else I can't do anything about.

However, after decades of practicing law and after years of defending lawyers, I have changed my mind and now believe that anti-lawyer jokes and polls stem more from matters within our control than from matters beyond our control. Although as individuals we can't do much about crooks, incompetents or other factors that discolor our reputation, one thing we can do is better serve clients and, remember, they are the ones who, for centuries, have bashed lawyers and perpetuated the negative stereotype that dogs us no matter how exemplary our individual conduct may be.

Think about it. Clients trust us with their secrets, safety, freedom, injuries, contracts, families, jobs, property and an enormous range of other individual, governmental and corporate interests and things can and often do go wrong during our pursuit of those objectives. Consequently, more than anybody else, clients sue us. More than anybody else, clients file bar complaints. More than anybody else, clients scorn us.

While continuing legal education, lawyer assistance programs and stricter ethical standards may improve our services, there is something more basic, perhaps more important, that we can do for our clients, our profession and ourselves. Recently, it is something I have tried to do myself and that is have better bedside manners.

THE COUNTRY DOCTOR

To explain what I mean by bedside manners, I must tell you about my father who was an old-fashioned, bag-toting general practitioner M.D. in rural Idaho whom I have written about in this and other magazines. *E.g., The New York Times Magazine* (July 7, 1991); *Newsweek* (December 16, 1996); *The Chicago Tribune Magazine* (December 24, 1995). He had no special training, he was not board certified in anything and his "residency," such as it was, had been as a World War II Army field surgeon during some of the bloodiest battles in the South Pacific.

The hospital where he practiced was small and basic; it had no departments of this or departments of that, no interns or residents, one operating room, one delivery room, a rudimentary laboratory, a limited number of beds and a non-state-of-the-art x-ray machine. In short, my father was the antithesis of many doctors today who, with their board certifications and sub-specialties and ICUs and MRIs and HMOs and emotional as well as physical detachments, care little about their patients and behave more like aloof technicians than as hands-on healers.

Given my father's professional limitations, he surely had patients who would have lived or who would have experienced better outcomes if his training and support had been stronger. Yet there were no doctor jokes in our little town. Medical malpractice actions were unthinkable. My father commanded more respect than did the clergy. To say he was thought of as God is overstating it but not by much.

The reason for all that esteem was not because he was the most accomplished doctor in the world because he wasn't and not because he cured all his patients because he didn't. The reason was simple: he cared constantly and authentically for his patients and they knew it, felt it and appreciated it. He cared by paying house calls, sometimes in the dead of winter, sometimes in the middle of the night, and sometimes to lumber camps high up in the mountains. He cared by making time for his patients and by knowing them and their families inside and out. And he cared in ways that, had I appreciated them earlier in my career, would have made me a better lawyer and, in some small measure, might have ennobled our profession.

WORDS

In my struggle to be that better lawyer, I realized that my vocabulary frequently kept me from thinking enough about those whom I represent. Compare the words my father used that focused him on internals with the words I use that focus me on externals.

My father inwardly "treated" patients and I outwardly "represent" clients. He "took histories" and I "gather facts." He spoke of "healing" and I talk of "winning." He worried about a patient's "candidacy" and I worry about a client's "claim." He referred to his cases by patient name and affliction, (*e.g.,* "Inez Nelson's heart condition") and I refer to my cases by legal problem as if it belonged to me (*e.g.,* "my securities case"). Without knowing it, he practiced an early version of what New-Agers might call "holistic medicine" and I don't practice anything that anybody would call "holistic law."

What this means is that, if I am to provide better bedside manners, I must breathe new life and instill deeper meaning into my vocabulary. Specifically, I have to "listen" more intently, "ask questions" more directly and "counsel" with greater sensitivity and straighter talk. That also means

I must borrow a medical exhortation my father slavishly lived by and that is this: "first, do no harm."

LISTENING

I regret to say this but, over the years, I have done less and less honest-to-goodness listening. For example, I can't listen when I am typing on my computer, shuffling papers, answering the telephone and putting someone else on hold and yet I've done just that. I can't listen when someone else is talking and all I'm doing is thinking about what I'm going to say as soon as I get the slightest chance to interrupt and I've done that too. Moreover, I can't listen when I'm talking at the same time as one, two or even three other people are also talking and that happens all the time.

What makes these ear-plugging incidents so unforgivable is that I am well practiced at being quiet and listening. In trials and depositions, I am tight-lipped and all ears. Why can't I do in my own office what I do in the courtroom or deposition room? Moreover, I'm always telling my clients and witnesses to concentrate on the questions being asked in court or depositions before uttering a peep. Why can't I do what I tell my own clients and witnesses to do? With better bedside manners maybe I can.

ASKING QUESTIONS

My father probably didn't realize it but he instinctively knew when to ask direct questions and when to ask leading questions. In conversations that I overheard when patients called our house, my father would ask direct questions at the outset, such as "how long is it between contractions?" or "what have you done for it?" Later on, when he had heard the patient out, he would switch to leading questions to get the details and ask questions such as "is it a sharp pain" or "do you feel faint when you stand up?"

By training and practice, I know all about direct questions and I'm careful, during trial, to ask my witnesses only direct questions when eliciting important information. I do that not only because the rules require it but also because it is far more effective for the witnesses to testify for themselves than for me to do it for them through leading questions.

Unfortunately, outside court I seem to forget all about using direct questions that will encourage clients or witnesses to tell me their truths in their own words. Instead, I pepper them with leading questions that tend to drag them away from their realities and toward my preconceived assumptions. That's not asking questions, that's manipulating and, to make matters worse, I am rarely conscious of it.

A related problem arises when I ask questions as if the colloquy were a one-time, static event. Yet, how many times have I finished an interview; had the client or witness verify the story in writing; later learned that the client or witness was honestly mistaken; and then watched them, on cross examination, made out to be liars because I had prematurely pinned them down to a story before all of the facts and documents had surfaced that could have refreshed their recollections and put things in proper sequence and perspective?

As I have discovered the hard way, past events are almost always reported incorrectly when recalled by raw memory alone. Consequently, to have better bedside manners, I must keep asking the same questions of the same clients and same witnesses as time passes and as information continues to develop. When I do that, I also must remember to listen, really listen, to what they tell me.

COUNSELING

I don't know how my father counseled patients because, except for overheard telephone conversations at home, I was not privy to those doctor-patient sessions. However, knowing him, I suspect that he was an intense listener, that he was compassionately blunt and that he often told patients to do nothing. I regret to admit it but that kind of counseling has frequently eluded me.

For years, I have "counseled" on the erroneous premise that "counseling" consisted more of my talking than my listening. When I did talk, it often came out as defensive hedging rather than comprehensible advice and, I'm embarrassed to say, that kind of mumbo jumbo has shown up hundreds of times in my "CYA" letters as well as in my one-on-one conversations. Like many other lawyers, I worry so much about being wrong, getting sued or scaring off clients that what I say or write is occasionally devoid of any meaning. A classic example is the jargonistic nonsense that all of us put into corporate audit responses.

In the absence of lay-it-on-the-line straight talk from lawyers, how can clients possibly give their "informed consent," especially to litigation? Often, when my cases finally end and the dust eventually settles and, using hindsight, the benefits are compared against the bruises, I wonder if I could have better warned clients at the outset how grueling, expensive, time-consuming, unpleasant and risky the whole undertaking was going to be.

Given the fact there is no way to forecast the future of any case or to warn clients of every risk, the best approach to pre-litigation counseling is probably to think as my father did and ascertain whether the client is a good "candidate" for litigation. If I think in terms of client "candidacy," I am more likely to cover vital issues and possible contingencies that are outside the narrow scope of the lawsuit.

Candidacy for individuals would include such subjects as age, health, finances, family circumstances, psychological strength, available time, and risk aversion. For example, how would a sick and infirm individual weather cross examination, delay, frustration and trial? How would the client cope if his or her good claim triggered a powerful counterclaim? What if the costs were to end up being greater than the benefits? Since the possibility of losing is omnipresent in every case, how would the client cope with defeat? Would psychological counseling, settlement, mediation or bankruptcy be a better alternative?

For corporations and government agencies, candidacy is also important.

Allegations and statements made in one case may conflict with allegations and statements made in other cases, SEC filings, regulatory reports and internal memos. A commonly forgotten question is whether the key witnesses will still be employed when their testimony will be needed and, if so, will they be happy people when that time comes? Also, what will former, sometimes disaffected employees in the "alumni association" have to say about the dispute? Will the litigation affect credit lines, bonding capacities, license restrictions, leases, marketing programs, mergers, acquisitions or legislative relations?

When counseling, one of the hardest things for lawyers to do is to tell clients to do nothing. Our livelihoods depend on our doing something and our instincts drive us to do something. No wonder that asking a lawyer if you need a lawsuit is sometimes like asking a barber if you need a haircut.

Just as my father had to tell patients with colds to stay in bed and do nothing, we must sometimes tell our clients the same thing because there are situations in which doing nothing is the right thing. The liability may exist but the damages may not. Tempers may cool. Threats may not be carried out. Markets may improve. Management might change. Statutes may be amended. Patience may be the right prescription.

DO NO HARM

For centuries, physicians have been taught a negative exhortation that lawyers should learn as well. In Latin, it is "Primum non nocere." In English, that means "First, do no harm." It was my father's credo.

Unfortunately, lawyers are prone to forget how much harm we can do even when our conduct is ethically sound, technically proficient and without a trace of malpractice. A common example is how competently and ethically handled divorce proceedings can produce enormous psychological, financial and familial harm. Thus, evaluating harm must always be an integral part of good bedside manners.

I don't know why it has taken me so many years to remember and adopt my father's bedside manners. If there is an answer to this question, it is probably found in this observation attributed to Mark Twain: "The older I got, the smarter my father became."

Printed in the United States
134960LV00002B/2/P

9 780881 001433